LORA WEBB NICHOLS

Homesteader's Daughter, Miner's Bride

LORA WEBB NICHOLS

Homesteader's Daughter, Miner's Bride

Compiled and written by
Nancy F. Anderson

from the personal papers of
Lora Webb Nichols

Foreword by Kathy Evertz
Cover painting by Jim Paxton
Cover design by Teresa Sales
All photographs are by Lora Webb Nichols,
unless otherwise noted

THE CAXTON PRINTERS, LTD.
Caldwell, Idaho
1995

Library of Congress Cataloging-in-Publication Data

Anderson, Nancy F. (Nancy Faye), 1936–
    Lora Webb Nichols : homesteader's daughter, miner's bride /
compiled and written by Nancy F. Anderson : from the personal papers
of Lora Webb Nichols.
        p.   cm.
    Includes index.
    ISBN 0-87004-368-4 (pbk. : alk. paper)
    1. Nichols, Lora Webb, 1883–1962. 2. Women--Wyoming--Biography.
3. Women--Wyoming--History--20th century. 4. Wyoming--Social life
and customs. 5. Wyoming--Biography.   I.   Title.
CT275. N62A53   1995
978.7'03'092---dc20
    [B]   95-41602
                                                          CIP

Lithographed and bound in the United States of America by
The CAXTON PRINTERS, Ltd.
Caldwell, Idaho 83605

For Lora,
Vera,
and all the other women who,
along with baling wire,
hold Wyoming together.

CONTENTS

ILLUSTRATIONS

FOREWORD

> In the privacy of their diaries, or in letters to trusted
> confidants, women have revealed what they "really
> felt," what they thought, believed, desired, or held
> important as they lived through the large events of
> history of the small rituals of daily life.[1]

In 1897, at the age of thirteen, Lora Nichols began
keeping a diary. For the next sixty-five years, she
devoutly, affectionately, and ceaselessly chronicled both
the ordinary and extraordinary incidents of her life in
diaries, letters, newspaper articles, photographs, and a
memoir. It is perhaps a gross understatement, then, to
refer to Lora Nichols as a born storyteller.

We are very fortunate that Nancy Anderson,
through her devotion, energy, and resolution to remain
faithful to the spirit and specifics of Lora's life, brings
Lora's remarkable story to us hers. In some ways, I
have come to view Nancy and Lora as collaborators:
both are eager to have us understand what Lora's life
was like, from the conditions of her everyday existence
(fording streams, riding her horse, living in a dirt-
floored cabin, excitedly preparing for holidays and
babies), to her dreams and aspirations, and certainly
her self-doubts and disappointments.

Lora delighted in and wondered at the world in which she lived. In this book we get a glimpse at the energetic, charming, and spirited ways in which she endeavored to participate fully in that world; we also see how she was sometimes frustrated in her attempts to do as she pleased, and how she felt about those restrictions, be they personal, marital, or cultural.

As a document of her inner life and daily experiences, this book will be of great interest to readers of women's history, women's work, women of the West, women's diaries and letters, and Wyoming history. But most of all, this book will captivate anyone who hopes to enter into the life of an amazing woman—a woman whose life was at once astonishingly different from and similar to our own. May the combined gifts of Lora Nichols and Nancy Anderson inspire others to edit and publish, when possible, other women's life-writings, and "intend always to keep a diary," as Lora promised herself—or write letters and take photographs, as a way to tell stories of our own lives. And may they encourage us to recognize that our lives, despite the sometimes unpredictable measure of highs and lows, are rich and wondrous, too.

Kathy Evertz
Laramie, Wyoming

[1]Cheryl Cline, *Women's Diaries, Journals, and Letters: An Annotated Bibliography.* New York: Garland Publishing, Inc., 1989, xi.

PREFACE

In our short span of life we humans can but take our place in the ever-changing tapestry of life, where the babies are being woven in at one extremity as the old folks are being ravelled out at the other. During our period of conscious life we do our best to "Walk in the Light" as this light is given to us. We are greatly influenced in this effort, especially in our young and formative years, by history, by tradition, by reminiscences and folk-tales of our parents, grandparents and associates. In thinking of my early childhood, I find that I was hardly able to see any difference in the things I actually experienced and the already accomplished deeds and facts of the past as discussed by my parents and their friends!

Lora Webb Nichols, 1883–1962

WHEN I BECAME ACQUAINTED WITH LORA in 1958, she was living in her Victorian house at Encampment, Wyoming. She was surrounded by her efforts to preserve "the tapestry of life" as she had received it from her progenitors and perceived it from her own life. During our early acquaintance, members of her family made casual references to "Mom's diaries." Imagining the usual, limited daily accountings of weather and incident, I found the originals as astounding as I was finding their author. Begun in April of 1897 when Lora was thirteen, the diaries extend from the childish, roughly created, variously papered books to the typed volumes of her adult years. The diaries involve a cast of hundreds and relate events from the most public to the most private. They include such diverse inserts as poems copied whole from books and magazines, recipes for photographic developing and toning solutions, lists of books borrowed and returned, music and lyrics of songs, and financial accountings. From the personally monumental to the mundane, the diaries document the entire life of a perceptive, passionate woman.

Augmenting the diaries are Lora's near sacred issues of *The Grand Encampment Herald*, which she at that time stored under her impressive old walnut bed. Using the editions of *The Herald*, her diaries and her own memories, Lora wrote *I Remember*, a book-length memoir. Beginning with family history, Lora follows the adventures of both grandfathers as participants in the movement west and as Civil War soldiers. Both become pioneer settlers in Boulder County, Colorado. From this point Lora's Great-Uncle Guy and Uncle Ezra of the Nichols' clan move north to Wyoming. Drawn to the isolated valley of the Grand Encampment River, they convince Horace, Lora's father, to homestead there. His homestead on the North Fork of the Grand Encampment becomes "the dear old ranch— Willow Glen" to Lora. It is the home of her childhood and coming of age and remains her place of solace and refuge for many years.

Life in the Grand Encampment Valley is disrupted, at the turn of the century, by an influx of speculators, prospectors, miners, and their attendant population. *I*

Remember, soon after its initial pages, evolves into a history of Grand Encampment City—the mining boom town platted the year that Lora began the diary, 1897. It becomes a history with only an occasional personal reference and concludes in 1905, the time when, for many of the "outlanders," the dream fades and new lodes elsewhere beckon.

While the diaries and the memoir are the major pieces in Lora's written legacy, there also are letters. Lora was an indefatigable correspondent. The early diaries record innumerable trips from the ranch to the post office with Lora noting what letters are sent and what received. Often a card or letter was copied in her diary; others were simply saved. One correspondence alone, that with an intelligent and articulate ranch woman, spans over twenty years and reads without pause because Lora saved not only Marguerite Peryam's letters, but also made copies of her own replies to complement them.

From the beginning, Lora's fervent, written documentation seems to reach toward an undefined audience. During her first winter as diarist, fourteen-year-old Lora plans,

> *I want to write a series of articles. "My Room." " In Our Pantry." " Wyoming pleasures." " Morning & Care," some Topics (Sun. Dec. 19. 1897).*

A few days later she confides,

> *I am going to try to be a little more graphic next year and go into more details if I do keep the paper-makers busy (Fri. Dec. 31, 1897).*

Selected family members had open invitations to read the diary, but it was much later that Lora briefly found her vehicles for public expression.

During the years 1929 and 1930, Emmett and M. Wesley Fuller published in Casper *The Pepper Pot* which they touted as "a strictly Wyoming product mainly for Wyoming people." While the twice-a-month magazine advocated the return of the public domain to the states, increased mineral development, and construction of a north-south railroad, it was, in addition, a literary magazine, featuring both poetry and prose. Numerous Encampment folk were published, but none more often than Lora Nichols. Her creative pieces in *The Pepper Pot* relied upon events from the diary for content and expression. The pieces fit effortlessly into the emerging popular genre dubbed "Western." Of Lora the editor wrote in the 2 June, 1929, issue,

> When I go down Encampment way, I'm going to have a visit with Lora Nichols . . . I know it will do my soul good to listen while she tells me about Wyoming, and life, and the way to contentment. Mrs. Nichols has genius—not merely talent. She has a genius for dreaming, and seeing, and interpreting.

Illustrating Editor Fuller's tribute is a photo of Lora with the credit "Photo by Rocky Mountain Studio, Encampment." Perhaps he was unaware that the proprietor of that studio was Lora herself, as he makes no mention of it in the profile. Yes, Lora's "ever-changing tapestry," not confined to her written words, also contains visual images. In 1899, for her sixteenth birthday, Lora's beau brought her a camera. That same year at Christmas, Pop ordered a developing outfit. Lora had another involvement as lifelong and ardently pursued as the writing of the diary. During our acquaintance,

Lora always was laden with her photographic paraphernalia, as were any who accompanied her. Her comment was, "I never know when I'll see the elephant." I don't recall a listing "elephant" in her negative file, but there are approximately 18,000 other listings. Beginning with her own incredible first recorded photograph "Mamma in the door," through the accumulations of her professional years, and increased by the work of others which she begged and borrowed (there is a collection of glass plates which she literally found), the catalog and corresponding negative files remain in Lora's own numerical system. Each photograph is identified absolutely as to time, place, and content.

Lora's house harbored the diaries, her negative file and its key, and the aged editions of the *Grand Encampment Herald*. There was also her extensive library, which included Twain and Dickens, Emerson, ancient and modern classics, westerns, popular fiction, and a nonfiction collection of myriad subjects. Lora read them all and quoted many. It became her habit to mark favorite passages with an *L* at the beginning and an *N* at the ending, forever personalizing her volumes for any future reader.

Augmenting her library was memorabilia of all sorts and sizes, thimble and desk, dish and lamp, rolling pin and walnut bed, each complete with a history, a myth, or both. Lora's diaries catalogue with detail the gifts she received for birthdays, Christmases, and other occasions for half a century. Yet, it was not mere possession which moved her. The significance and the circumstance of each gift also became part of her tapestry.

Why was Lora so determined to define her world: her time, her place, and her role in the complexity of things? Why did she leave her mark in such a variety of tangible ways?

Lora states simply that she, like the rest of her classmates in Boulder, began to keep a diary. Whether this was the result of a teacher's assignment or one of those often inexplicable, adolescent epidemics, Lora doesn't reveal. However, the turn of the century was an age of biography; memoirs of the Civil War and the Indian conflicts, including accounts by captives, were popular reading. History was as yet defined by the exploits of the individual. In a democratic thrust, women could emerge as self-defined heroines.

Lora is, indeed, the heroine of her first diary describing the family's wagon journey return to Wyoming. These early entries contain elements of many a classic western travel journal of her day: tearful farewell to remaining family, detaining snowstorm, raging spring torrents, and balky horses. In each case, Lora remains her papa's steadfast, supportive companion. From this beginning, Lora was propelled into the role of diarist for sixty-five years.

Lora's parents provided a nurturing ambiance for her early efforts. They provided inspiration through their own participation in and respect for the oral tradition. They applauded her attempts at self-education and creativity. They had more practical concerns. Despite the small space of the homestead cabins and the immensity of the ranch work, Sylvia and Horace blessed young Lora with privacy and time.

While her spirit could be released by the diary, without photography, Lora still would have been consigned to the roles of rancher's daughter, young bride and mother, all within the circumferences prescribed by the community. The Kodak became an instrument of physical liberation. Most importantly, Lora's photography gave her an assigned, recognized role in the new diversity created by the booming atmosphere of the valley. During the heyday of the Grand Encampment Mining District, the camera guaranteed her access to the claims and the mines, the tram stations, the smelter. It was her entry to the tie camps and river drives. Among her earliest negatives, the many portraits of women, children, and babies are joined by those of teamsters, miners, ranchers and homesteaders, valley pioneers, and saloon keepers.

As confidante, Diary was the recipient of Lora's innermost thoughts. It heard her confessions of self-doubt and self-condemnation and recorded her resolutions for the achievement of grace. It received the full fury of her rages and her tears of frustration (at times literally on the page). It shared dreadfully "shocking," in her word, improprieties about topics then banned from polite society. And during all this, there is another Lora who seems to stand aside and view her own antics, predicaments, joys, and tragedies with an objective, documentary eye.

This is one of the qualities which Lora holds in common with her Wyoming literary contemporary Elinore Pruitt Stewart. The objective eye elevates Stewart's letters and accounts and Lora's myriad written expressions; neither is mere feminine, rural reminiscence of the West. The Valley of the Green and the North Fork of the Encampment are their settings, but their plots are as old as the drama of womankind.

Given the plethora of material, in editing I have endeavored to follow guidelines. My primary purpose is to allow Lora to speak for herself. This is an easy task in Part I which is taken from her volume *I Remember* with a few pertinent additions from the diaries and letters; here, Lora is her own narrator. Part 2 is an edited collage of passages from the diaries, *I Remember*, and other sources. I beg the reader's pardon for my necessary interference in Part 2 of Lora's saga. In all cases, Lora's words and punctuations are preserved, as is the integrity of her observation.

The selections focus on Lora, her maturation and her adaptation to the variety of roles demanded and offered her. Good diaries, by definition, often contain a hundred stories not necessarily about the premier player; where there is a conclusion to one of these stories, I have tried to include it for the edification of the reader; where there is not, we must all remain in wonder. Diaries include the earth-shattering and the trivial. In following general themes, I, doubtless, quote both. There are, however, those passages of sheer beauty or depth of expression which, somehow, have found their way single-handedly into the edited narrative. In conclusion, my purpose is, to use Lora's metaphor, to prove that "the tapestry" of reality contains colors more vibrant and textures more tactile than any fiction can create.

Nancy F. Anderson

ACKNOWLEDGEMENTS

THE WYOMING COUNCIL FOR THE HUMANITIES, through their Speakers' Bureau, first presented Lora to the people of Wyoming. Speaking as Lora, I took her diary and photographs on the road with a most capable crew: The late Jimmy Kitching of Hanna on banjo; his wife, Muriel as promptor; my husband Victor as chauffeur and technician; and Carol Boam Smith as substitute. In over one hundred performances state-wide, Lora's lively commentary and accompanying photos enchanted audiences of all ages.

During 1990, the Council, continuing its interest in Lora's legacy, awarded me a Centennial Grant; this book is the result. I am endebted to JoAnn Richardson of Elk Mountain, Denice Wheeler of Evanston, and John T. Schwartz of Wilson for their perceptive comments on part or all of the manuscript and to Pam Hardenbrook, editor at The Caxton Printers, Ltd., for her capable, collegial assistance with the total project. The superb illustrations, so integral to the narrative, were reproduced by the Ludwig Studio of Laramie. Kathy Evertz of Laramie, serving as mentor and muse, led me to discover anew the uniqueness and beauty of Lora's expression.

Vera Oldman, Lora's daughter-in-law, was with me every word of the way. As the long-time President of the Board and Curator of the Grand Encampment Museum, Inc. at Encampment, Wyoming, Vera was a magical, inexhaustible resource on family and town history.

Together, we celebrate Lora.

ABBREVIATIONS

GEH *Grand Encampment Herald*

IR *I Remember,* Book–length memoir by Lora Webb Nichols

+ (Or multiples thereof preceding dates of diary entries) Signify days "missed" since Lora's last entry.

Part I

Lora's Narrative

A GIRL'S–EYE VIEW OF EARLY DAYS
IN THE ROCKY MOUNTAINS

HAVE YOU EVER RIDDEN, preferably horse-back, along the sage covered foot-hills of Wyoming's Rocky Mountains? Some of my earliest childhood memories were established against such a back-ground; wagon roads connected the widely scattered ranches, just two parallel paths with high sage-brush between and on both sides. If a rancher, going visiting, with his wife beside him on the high spring-seat and his children on quilts in the wagon bed back of it, should meet another such vehicle it was necessary, in order to pass, that each turn his team out into the sage-brush. The smell of freshly crushed sage is like nothing else in the world; if you have ever smelled it, you know what I mean. Perhaps the clear tangy mountain air, and even the roadside dust, adds to my nostalgic memory of Wyoming sage! My mother told me that when she first came to Wyoming she contracted a bad case of so-called "Mountain Fever," which very frequently put a tender-foot to bed for weeks, or even months. The native's sovereign remedy for this malady was sage-brush tea, a strong infusion of the young green tips of sage (and a very distasteful drink it was, as I well remember); she says she drank so many *quarts* of the stuff that it was two years after her recovery before she could endure having Dad "turn out" to pass a team without the smell of the crushed sage making her deathly sick. I can remember her saying to Dad if we saw a team coming our way, "Now Horace, *don't* stop to talk, will you? You can call back to them after we get back in the road."

WHICH PASSES NO MAN BY

The victim has the backache,
The stomach ache, a pain—
He goes to bed almost half dead,
With no hope to rise again.

His brow is hot, he's most forgot
His name, or cares a wee;
His eyes are hazed, his brain is crazed
But still soaks in sage tea.

Sage tea, O my, sage tea, O me,
Drink, and drink, and drink;
'Tis awful stuff, its mighty rough,
But it saves them from the brink.

The malady transforms the saint
Into a disbeliever;
But after all there's no excuse—
It's only mountain fever.

You laugh at him, once full of vim,
Now meek, so weak, so shy;
But mind you, all ye tenderfeet—
You'll have it by and by.

Earle R. Clemens
(GEH/IR 111)

I think I was about eight when Dad first called my attention to the old Cherokee Trail; he and I were out together that day, horseback, riding out to a ranch on Indian Creek and he said to me, "Notice anything queer or different about this road?

"Yes, it doesn't have any sage-brush in the middle."

"Did you ever wonder why?"

"Yes. Do *you* know?" One of my greatest pleasures was having Dad "explain" things I did not understand, and I never forgot what he had to say that day about the Cherokee Trail. Turning in his saddle he called my attention to the trail plainly marked across the entire valley from the Cow Creek mesa where it crossed to the west of the ranch on top of the mesa which was, in later years developed by Charles D. Terwilliger; from there it came through the Charles T Fait Ranch, the old Wolfard Ranch, and crossed the Grand Encampment River at the present town of Riverside, in Carbon County Wyoming. From this point to Indian Creek it was for many years the wagon road in common use, and it was along this part Dad and I were riding. He said the trail was made by the Cherokee Indians, "Not war parties, but when they were moving camp, with the squaws and papooses along and all their ponies." He said the braves rode ahead, driving any loose horses before them, and the squaws came behind, with their blankets and few cooking pots carried in bundles lashed onto a cross pole between two other poles with the brush tops still attached. These side poles were lashed one on either side of a pony, the cross pole with bundles just back of his tail and the brush ends dragging the ground. No wonder the Cherokee Trail was *bare* with all that traffic! The Grand Encampment River received its name because of the Indians holding an annual grand encampment on its banks.

THE TAPESTRY OF LIFE

ALL FOUR OF MY GRANDPARENTS CAME "across the plains" in covered wagons, and all settled in Boulder County, Colorado: David Hanson Nichols with his wife and two sons arrived at Boulder in 1859 and settled there on farm land. It was here that his only daughter was born in 1866 and this was his home until his death in 1900. The farm was gradually sold, a few acres at a time, and is long since a part of the city of Boulder.

During the war, Captain David H. Nichols commanded Company D of the Third Colorado Cavalry, and during his military service his company fought four battles with the Indians, one of them being that of "Sand Creek" which will be remembered as a most sanguinary engagement.

Many a time I heard my Grandfather say, emphatically, "The only *good* Indian is a dead Indian." His experiences with the "Noble Red Man" had, very understandably, prejudiced him against them although I have often heard him say when visiting with his cronies, "Considering the treatment the Indians got from the white men, it is no wonder they showed no mercy." I do not like to remember the anecdotes they told about Indian atrocities, which were too awful to bear contemplation. Sometimes my Grandmother would make a sign to remind him that we children were listening and he would, without any obvious check in his conversation, switch right over to anecdotes concerning Indians that were really funny, thus giving us youngsters something pleasant to think about.

I remember the first one he swung into one afternoon, (after a particularly horrible story of torture) was still connected with the army and his life in camp: it seems that he had an air mattress in his camp equipment, and there was one old squaw, who was always hanging around camp begging, who was absolutely fascinated by that mattress, having seen it blown up for use and then deflated later for packing. She was forever sneaking around and turning the valve, screaming with joy when the escaping air began to whistle. Of course somebody would chase her out of camp and shut it off again, but Grandfather said, "It was mighty hard to get a real sleep on that thing." He would come in exhausted, throw himself down and drop asleep almost immediately, only to be awakened by the whistling air, and see the old gal beating it for shelter. "Damn her, she knew I'd *skin* her if I could catch her!"

Another of his stories that my brother and I giggled over for many a day was about a group of Indian children who were playing on top of a steep little grass covered hill; one little boy got hold of something to eat, which he refused to share, but set himself firmly down on top of the hill and started eating; the others kept milling around, whooping and scuffling as usual, until two boys came past him, from behind, each grabbing one of his ankles as they passed and dragging him swiftly down the hill! Most of the Indian children wore literally *no* clothing, and, said Grandfather, "I'll bet his tail burned!"

Often Grandfather would drive up town in the phaeton, driving "Old Doc," the family steed that my brother used to refer to as "a large red horse with square corners." Sometimes he would take my brother and me along; it was lots more fun than driving out in the family carriage, the surrey, yes, literally "The Surrey with the Fringe on Top," as it was really cosy in the phaeton with just Grandfather and we could coax him to sing Indian songs, or talk in one of the two Indian languages with which he was familiar. We often begged him to give an Indian War Whoop, and one day when we were quite out of town for several miles, he *did*! We were both begging him, "*Don't* do that any more Grandpa." Of all the unearthly sounds I ever heard I never heard another that made my scalp prickle like that one did. Ever afterward, when we teased Grandfather beyond his patience, he would say, "Don't you want me to War Whoop?"

"No, Grandpa, *no!*"

My maternal grandfather, George Washington Wilson, did not "go west" until after the close of the Civil War. He was born November 13, 1828, near the village of Laurens, Otsego County, New York. He was raised on a farm, and like many another young man of his era, developed into a "floater," a drifter, a Jack-of-all-trades, traveling around the eastern states as his fancy dictated, working at whatever job was available when he ran short of money, but having no definite plan for the future.

I never saw Grandfather Wilson, but family tradition pictures him as a small man, 5 feet 7 inches in height, fair, with bright blue eyes. As a care-free, happy-go-lucky he was no doubt attractive to girls. He certainly did prove attractive to one girl! She was a serious minded young woman, two years older than he, who was a professor of languages in a high school in Pennsylvania when they met. After a whirl-wind courtship they were married, on March 24, 1853.

This maternal grandmother of mine seems to have been quite a person! Her father, Andrew Peck, and his four brothers were all Methodist ministers. She had the best education available to women in the United States at that time, and her family was very much averse to her marrying this attractive stranger. They felt that her education and opportunities were being thrown away. Her very position as a teacher of languages was considered quite an achievement "for a woman" in those early days when very, very few women did any kind of work out of their homes. But Miss Betsy Peck evidently had a will of her own, and in spite of all opposition they were married, and she joined him in his wandering life, until her early death sixteen years later.

Their first child, Leonard Wesley Wilson was born April 27, 1854, somehere in the state of New York; the second child, Nancy Lucena Wilson, was born December 9, 1856, in Harrison County Penn; the third child, Sylvia Maria Wilson was born December 27, 1861, at West Eaton New York.

Grandfather Wilson volunteered, soon after the opening of the Civil War, his wife, Leonard and Sylvia going back to the home of the Peck family and Nancy being placed in the home of a wealthy family who was interested in her, and where she remained until the war was over. In speaking of his war experiences, Grandfather always mentioned with pride that he had *volunteered.* He was not in any battles, his regiment being on guard duty. He was a member of Company E,

Eleventh Minnesota Volunteer Infantry, and was sent to Nashville, Tennessee to guard supply trains, his "beat" being between Nashville and Chattanooga.

It was soon after the close of the war that he assembled his wife and three children and started west, joining a wagon train. The rigors of a pioneer life were too much for my grandmother who had never been exposed to any hardship, and her health began to fail. They stopped for a time in Minnesota, and it was here that the fourth child, William Towne Wilson was born, March 2, 1868, at Elgin. As soon as grandfather felt that the child and his ailing mother could endure the hardships of trail life, the journey was resumed. Their next stop was Missouri, where grandmother died, April 4, 1869, when the baby was only a little over a year old.

Grandfather and his four motherless children stayed in Missouri four years, before coming to Colorado. My mother [Sylvia], who was seven when her mother died, said she did not remember much about the four years in Missouri, but can remember clearly the journey by wagon across the plains, and the great herds of buffalo. The wagon train was sometimes obliged to halt while a large herd traveled across the plain in front of them.

Grandfather kept the family together until they reached Colorado; Uncle Leonard worked as a carpenter helping to build the station on the Colorado Southern Railroad at Niwot, Colorado, where grandfather was the first station agent, moving there in 1875. Uncle Leonard, who was then twenty-one, did not stay at home much after that, and Aunt Nancy was married October 28, 1875, to Platt A. Hinman.

Grandfather never re-married; Mother said he often said to his girls, "You needn't worry. I'll never put a step-mother over you." She and her sister, my Aunt

Nan, used to giggle together about it and say to each other, "No, of course he won't; nobody'd have him!" It seems he was quite strict with his children and they stood greatly in awe of him, but after his girls were grown up and married, they realized that there were women in the neighborhood who would gladly have married him! It was just a deep conviction on his part that his children ought not to be afflicted by a step-mother.

Grandfather used to say that he did not want any daughter of his to have to marry for a home. In those days an unmarried woman was sort of on a "poor rela-tion" basis; probably living with a married sister or brother, taking care of their children and feeling defi-nitely superfluous. No wonder they sometimes con-tracted unwise marriages to escape from this position and have a home of their own! He taught both girls the use of the telegraph instrument, my mother becoming an expert operator. In this way he provided his daugh-ters with a means of livelihood in the event of their not marrying or of losing their husbands. Good telegraph operators were always in demand. As it happened nei-ther girl had to depend on this skill for a living, but my mother made some use of it during her school days, when she was attending high school and the University of Colorado at Boulder.

Her employer was a Mr. Lewis, Station Agent at the Boulder depot and at this time she was boarding at the home of my paternal grandparents, Captain and Mrs. DH Nichols. She would go home to Niwot each week-end, do up the house-work for Grandfather Wilson and her young brother Will, then go back to school again Monday morning on the train. Her work with Mr. Lewis was after school hours Monday through Friday.

She became very fond of Captain and Mrs. Nichols, and they of her; Grandfather began calling her "daughter," long before she became his daughter-in-law, and continued to do so as long as he lived. Grandmother called her "Sylph," the nick-name fastened upon her by some member of the family, probably Franc, the only daughter who was five years her junior, and whose room she shared. Franc was fourteen years younger than her brother Horace, and sixteen years younger than the elder brother Ezra.

I think it was during the winter of 1878–79 that my mother first met Horace, whom she later married. He had just returned from a trip to Wyoming to see his brother Ez and a young uncle, Guy H Nichols, who had settled in the valley of the Encampment River in southern Wyoming, after having decided that North Park, in northern Colorado, was too severe a climate. Uncle Guy and Uncle Ez had intended to take up land in North Park, near the present town of Walden, and had spent the previous winter there. They liked the Encampment valley so much they kept writing to my Dad to come on up and take up a homestead near them. So Dad had been up to see the country.

Uncle Guy, who was a younger brother of my Grandfather Nichols, was only a comparatively few years older than Uncle Ez and my father, and they had worked and played together during the years when "the Nichols boys" were growing up. They hauled freight, with ox teams, from Denver to Cheyenne; they worked together in the coal mines, and at one time, John Cluff and Will Peryam (both of whom later settled in the Encampment valley) worked with them. My father and Will Peryam were class-mates for a time at the University of Colorado. Uncle Guy and Uncle Ez decided they would go "up north" and investigate the

Encampment valley, where it was reported, there was plenty of good land to be homesteaded, plenty of game, plenty of wood.

When my father got back to Boulder that winter of 1878–9, he was very enthusiastic about the opportunities "up north," but as events transpired he did not go up there to stay until 1884. You see there was this charming young Sylvia Wilson, and getting that girl for his wife suddenly became the most important thing in life! During the next winter, 79–80, Dad got himself a good job as a guard at the Colorado State Penitentiary at Canyon City, and began urging an immediate marriage. My mother was attending the University, and wanted to finish out her year there, so Dad finally had to agree to that.

"Well, all right then; when school's out you come on down to Canyon and we'll be married. I've got a house, up close to Porter's and by that time, I can pick up enough furniture to get along on till you can come down and choose your own."

But then and there he struck a snag! Said my mother, with her little chin in the air, "I am not going *to* any town to any man I'm not married to; if you want me you'll have to come back and get me."

This conversation took place in early January of 1880. Dad said he did not believe he could get any time off to come up and get her, but she could not bear to give up her school and marry him at once as he urged. He had to leave for Canyon City on January 21, and finally he entered into a conspiracy that he hoped might work; it did.

Mother was still working occasional odd hours at the depot for Mr. Lewis. Dad went around and told Mr. Lewis the whole story, and how he just couldn't go and leave her unmarried, for he was sure somebody else would grab her before he could get back! Mr. Lewis had a properly sympathetic attitude and suggested Dad better just marry her, right now; he suggested that Dad go up to the University and leave a message for her "Mr. Lewis wants to see you after school." Of course she would just think Mr. Lewis had some work for her, and he said if Dad would get the preacher and have him over at the church, he, Mr. Lewis, would guarantee to bring Miss Sylvia right over there as soon as she appeared.

"Then" said he, "it's up to you."

When my sister and I were children, there was nothing we enjoyed more than getting Dad and Mother to tell us stories about what happened when they were young; our romantic little-girl hearts were especially pleased if we could get Mother to "tell about when you were married, Mamma, *please!*" because she would turn pink and Dad would sit and twinkle his eyes at her, and when she got to the part of her story where "Mr. Lewis said, 'You and I have a short call to make first, around the corner here; come on.' and when we turned the corner, there at the church door was the minister and beside him, Dad, with his eyes sticking out till you could have knocked them off with a stick."

Dad would interrupt and say, "Why don't you tell the girls what you said?" but she would never tell us! Dad would say, "No wonder my eyes stuck out; I didn't know whether she'd shoot me, or marry me."

And Mother would continue her story by saying, "Well, I suddenly decided I *would* marry him; Mr. Lewis was the best man and when it came to the part of the ceremony where the minister said, 'With this ring I thee wed,' Mr. Lewis said to Dad, 'Give me that ring you have on your finger,' and then he handed it right back to Dad saying, 'This will answer the purpose.'" and she was accordingly "wed" with the aid of a handsome cameo! It seems Dad had forgotten in his excitement to provide a wedding ring, and Sis and I always loved the fact that she would never let him buy her another ring.

She would say, "This is the ring I was married with, and it *is* my wedding ring."

Dad always looked a little shame-faced over that, but he would turn the ring on her finger; as the cameo side appeared on top he would say, "This is her engagement ring, and when you turn it on around, (suiting the action to the word, so that it appeared a plain gold band) *"this* is her wedding ring."

I think this was our favorite part of the wedding story, although we liked to hear Dad go on to tell how, when they got home that evening (it was Monday, so of course "home" meant *his* home where she boarded during the week) he wanted to introduce her to his mother as "my wife." My mother used to say that she wished she had let him do that, because when school was out in the spring, and she was preparing to leave, she had to tell his mother about it without his supporting presence. However, Grandmother took the news quite calmly, saying, "Well, I thought it might be that way."

Canyon City was my parents' home for the next three years; it was here that my only brother, Guy Clifford Nichols, was born, October 11, 1880, and also my only sister, Lizzie May Nichols, February 25, 1882. Before my own arrival in this "vale of tears" (as the old phrase went, but I prefer "vale of laughter" which seems just as logical; at least I have found it so), they had returned to Boulder where my Nichols grandparents had arranged for Dad to buy two–and–a–half acres of land from them, and a small brick house was built on it. My grandparents were very fond of Mother, and wanted the family near them; no doubt they, like grandparents the world over, thought the grandchildren were wonderful!

My dad had to endure a good bit of good-natured "ribbing" about a statement he had made, before he had any children; it seems he had a strong objection to children being named after their parents or grandparents; he said, "I'm not going to make tomb-stones out of *my* kids!" Well, maybe not, but he named his son Guy after his favorite uncle, Guy H Nichols, and a boy-hood pal, Clifford Turner! Then, his daughter was named Lizzie for his mother, not Elizabeth, but Lizzie as his mother was called and the middle name, May, was my mother's suggestion. It was only a few months before my birth that Dad gave up his work as guard at the pen, and I have heard him tell how he came to select my name, Lora. The stone wall around the prison was a high one, and all the way around there were towers at close intervals; every guard walked a beat between two towers, and was expected to keep a close watch on the enclosed area at all times. They could spend a few minutes in each tower if the weather was cold or stormy, as each tower had a window overlooking the Yard, and had also been equipped with a wooden box which could be used as a seat. The box in one of Dad's towers was a packing case for a brand of laundry soap called "Colorado's Best" and was considerably scarred by notches and scrolls carved by some previous guard or guards; The *CO* had been whittled off of the beginning of the word Colorado, and the *DO* off the ending, leaving the letters *LORA*, and Dad said to himself, "If my baby is a girl, I am going to call her Lora"—and she *was* and he *did*!

This name met with my mother's approval, as my sister's name had done, and again she selected the middle name, Webb; Mr. Webb was a very good friend of the family, a teacher in the Boulder schools. He was very pleased when told that Mother had named her baby after him and he told her he had five namesakes, and four of them were girls.

Grandfather Wilson, who was still station agent at Niwot, had no association with the family at this time; he had utterly forbidden my mother to marry Dad, and promptly "disowned" her when she did! He once sent her a message saying that he would be glad to see *her* at any time, but she promptly sent back word, "I do not care to visit where my husband and children are not welcome."

PLENTY OF GOOD LAND TO BE HOMESTEADED, PLENTY OF GAME, PLENTY OF WOOD

ON OCTOBER 28, 1883, I was born at the little brick house in Boulder, being the first one of the grandchildren that Dad's mother had welcomed into the world; it was only about a year later that Uncle Guy and Uncle Ez finally persuaded Dad that he would always regret it if he did not get himself a ranch in Wyoming!

Grandmother was not a bit happy about having Dad move his family so far away. As we were making the move by team and wagon, taking some household goods with us, Grandma finally persuaded Mother and Dad to leave my brother Cliff with her until the following year when she expected to pay the Wyoming relatives a visit. She felt that Mother would have enough with two little girls on her hands for such a trip. So that was the way it was done. My brother was four years old at the time; for some reason, I really do not know what, the proposed visit of Grandmother the following year did not take place; the next year Cliff was six and entered school in Boulder, and he continued to make his home with my grandparents.

Both uncles were married by this time. It was in the old coal town of Carbon, which is near Hanna, Wyoming, that Uncle Guy and Uncle Ez first encoun-

The little brick house in Boulder, where Lora was born

tered a peppy Irish widow, named Maggie Culleton, who was running a boarding house. The widow had at that time, six children, Johnny, Jim, Ben, Pierce, and "Doc," and their sister Katie. My mother told me that when news of the weddings of Uncle Guy and Maggie and Uncle Ez and Katie reached Boulder, Grandfather Nichols said, "Well, I thought Ez might marry the girl, but I didn't know Guy was going to marry the widow."

Uncle Guy and Uncle Ez and their families were very much a part of my life in those early years after we came to Wyoming, and some of my happiest hours were spent in their company. I can still visualize my dear old Uncle Guy—the nearest thing to a grandfather that my life up to nine years held—as he moved about the house, or sat in his big rocker in the corner;

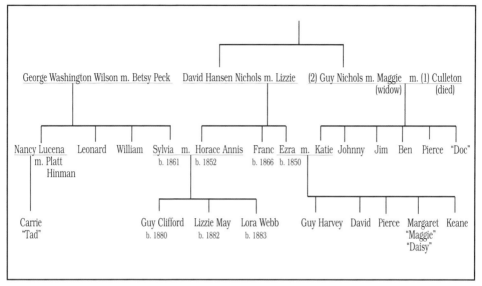

Lora's family

and Aunt Maggie, the cantankerous old Irish gal who was a stormy petrel indeed, but big hearted withal.

It was always a big event when we visited at Uncle Guy's. I can remember so well, Uncle Pierce making lemonade for us and the cousins, and drawing up that ice cold water from the old stone well for that purpose—it is really a wonder I did not drown in that well, I was so fascinated by it, and used to lean over and admire my moonfaced and pigtailed image until I was snatched back by some irate relative! Sometimes Uncle Johnny was home from some wild jaunt, maybe clear to Carbon, even! On one never-to-be-forgotten trip he gave me a tame rate, said his mother did not like it, whereupon Aunt Maggie gave a mighty snort and slapped the biscuit dough on the board with undue vigor, and my own mother looked far from happy. I could write a story of the doings of the same rat, really! [Letter to George Peryam, Thursday, February 17, 1949]

Uncle Guy had promised Dad "a place to live until you get your land and a house built on it," and we were very comfortably established in a warm building, right by Uncle Guy's own house. These pioneer houses were built of material from the native forests, the men cutting the trees, sawing them into suitable lengths for house logs, then hauling them to their newly acquired ranches and building their own houses. The walls were made of logs, laid one on top of the other, notched at the corners to make the logs lie as close together as possible, then the spaces between were "chinked" and daubed with plaster. The resulting building was a good warm shelter against the wintry blizzards; the roof was made of smaller poles, and covered with a good thick layer of earth. Some of the houses had floors of such lumber as could be secured, some had no floor other than the hard packed earth, and within my memory there were still a few "puncheon" floors, made by sawing thin "slices" from the logs and placing the resulting two inch discs side by side until the floor space was covered, then filling in the spaces with earth.

The so-called shanty of Uncle Guy, where we spent the first winter or two, had no floor, but there were tanned deer hides spread all over it. These were tanned with the hair on, and made very acceptable carpets. It was just one large square room, equipped with a cook stove in the center, and a homemade table, beds, and chairs. It was built into the side of a steep bank, beside the creek; this had a double advantage as the bank gave extra warmth and protection from the wind, and the water for household use was right at the door. The door was made of heavy boards, unplaned, and equipped with a homemade wooden latch operated by a buckskin thong passed through a small hole bored in the door. Truly "the latchstring is out" was a literal phrase of welcome! If any timid lady had to stay alone with her children while the menfolk were off on roundup or something, she could pull that latchstring through the hole into the cabin and behold, her door was locked and nobody could come in! My own mother was a good pioneer wife as she was not in the least timid.

The shanty had one window, a "half-sash" on the side toward the bank (from the outside the window was just even with the ground) and from the window one looked right at the store which was across the wagon road from Uncle Guy's house. This was a general store as the sign stated, and was also the post office of Swan, Wyoming of which Uncle Guy was postmaster.

It was in the late '70s or early '80s that the last "Indian scare" occurred, as I remember my relatives talking about it; there had been one or two previous scares and many settlers had taken their wives and families to Fort Fred Steele for safety. Of course there were stories of how the Indians burned buildings and destroyed crops, as well as carrying off all livestock. The log house Uncle Guy built on his ranch was equipped with loop-holes through which to fire on marauding redskins.

Uncle Guy's log house had a meat pole which stuck up at the corner of the stone milk house (which was constructed by my Uncle Ez, a stonemason). This very tall pole was equipped with a rope and pulley like a flagstaff. The fresh meat was hoisted to the top of the pole, "above the flies," they said, and there it "kept" miraculously. As mealtime approached, Aunt Maggie would cast a look at Uncle Doc or Uncle Pierce, her two sons who were at home, and he would go out and let down the meat, slicing off what was needed, and hoist it to safety again.

In those days there was an abundance of wild game and so never a shortage of fresh meat. My mother used to wish occasionally for some beef, but no one wanted to butcher any beef, they were growing into valuable property! I remember Dad bringing home a nice roast of beef one day when he had been down to the store; it seems someone had butchered, and Uncle Guy remembered Mother's wishes for some beef, and she was disappointed in the result. It was tough and she was royally laughed at by all the friends and neighbors in a good-natured way, for a long time. They told her she had just forgotten how much tenderer the wild game was than "bully beef."

A H Huston, pioneer rancher on Cow Creek who was a crack shot, used to have a lot of fun occasionally furnishing meat for all the families up and down the Encampment and Cow Creek. Herds of antelope were quite frequent on the flats between the Encampment and Indian Creek, occasionally a herd of elk would come down there out of the mountains if feed got short. Mr. Huston and one of his older sons, John or Len, would hook a good team onto a bobsled and drive out there, within shooting distance, then the son would drive, as Mr. Huston shot as many as the sled would carry. Then they would drive down the river and leave a "carcass" for everyone who was getting short of meat. I have heard Uncle Ez tell many a time what a sight it was to see the Hustons, both standing up in the bobsled as it wildly careened in pursuit of the herd. But Uncle Ez said, "He mowed 'em down."

I can remember at our first home on the ranch, the homestead cabin, when Dad would go out to milk, just at dusk, I was always tagging along. If our meat supply was getting low, Dad would take his gun with him, set it down by the bars and start milking. Looking at the horizon, he could see deer, coming down to the stream to drink; Dad would wait until he saw one that looked young and fat, then he would stop milking, take up his gun, go and shoot the deer, whoop for Mother to come out and finish milking that cow while he dressed out the meat.

My parents and their friends and neighbors lived a really rugged life, but as a child, I was conscious only of the warm enfolding love surrounding me, and had no feeling of fear or worry. Ah, "God's in his heaven, all's right with the world"—indeed, when a family unit is as close and cozy as ours I can visualize those winter evenings, by the roaring wood fire: Dad, Mother, my sister, and I. Sometimes the parents were reading, quietly and we girls playing on the floor with our toys, dolls of course and the most amazing doll furniture constructed by Dad! We always liked the furniture Dad made best of all, even though our grandparents in Boulder, Colorado had sent each of us and Uncle Ez's girls, a dear little doll dresser with a mirror. Sometimes we all four played games, and Dad was a master at evolving games out of the material at hand. The very first little thing I ever remember Dad making for me— Mother said I was four at the time—was a paper windmill. I had been confined to the house for several days with a bad cold and when Dad came in from his chores and sat down by the kitchen stove to talk to Mother as she was cooking supper, I went and climbed up in his lap, feeling very sorry for myself. A smile and a hug from Dad could make even a sick little girl happy. He took one look at me, and asked my sister to bring him a piece of Mother's note paper, the scissors, a pin, and a stick of kindling. Then he made a windmill, fastening it on the stick. He got an especially long pin, bent it at the right angles and fastened it in a joint of the stovepipe where the rising heat made it whirl merrily. I went to sleep watching it.

It was on a winter evening much later than that one, when Sis and I were clamoring for "something to do," Mother made some mention of wishing we had some games, "Tiddlywinks or something." Whereupon Dad snapped his fingers, winked, and Sis began laughing because she knew he was going to evolve something. Sis always got to help with these mighty projects; this time he sent her for a blanket, which he folded over twice and put it on his smoker's stand, which was an oblong table about eighteen by thirty inches. Then he requisitioned a little round deep wicker basket that Mother kept buttons in, emptied out the buttons, and put the basket up on the table. Next he selected half-a-dozen flat white pearl buttons, about half inch in diameter, and an equal number of smoked pearl in the same size. Then he choose two large buttons, coat size, about one and a half inches and behold we played tiddlywinks, Dad and I partners against Mother and Sis. Those big buttons made dandy shooters and how the small ones did hop on that blanket; we had to calm down our enthusiasm considerably before we could get the buttons to hop into the basket instead of way off the table.

We used to play card games a great deal too; sometimes the four of us playing high five, or two of us playing cribbage. I did not realize until many years later that Dad was teaching me arithmetic with the aid of cribbage. Very occasionally, our only close neighbors would come over in the evening and the adults would play cards while we four children played at other games. This was the Cluff family, Mr. & Mrs. John Cluff and their two sons, Chet and Ez, Chet being about a year older than my sister Lizzie, and Ez a few months younger than I.

Most of the winter evenings from the time we were girls were old enough to enjoy it, we spent reading aloud, Dad and Mother taking turns at reading a chapter each, Sis joining in a very early age, as she read well, and eventually even I. However the evenings I remember most clearly were before I had much of a hand in the actual reading. Books were scarce in those early days, and we soon read aloud all that Mother and Dad owned and many that were loaned to us by Will Peryam, who like my own parents was and avid reader. How delighted my parents were when they came into possession of a full set of the "Works of Charles Dickens." They were paper bound. Dad got them from some man who was at Swan Store one day, and said that he was going to discard them. Well, that set of Dickens was like a gold mine to my parents, and it was reading aloud from Dickens *every* evening that winter! 1891–2, I believe. Mother told me many, many years later that it was during this period that she and Dad first realized that the children were really *listening* to the stories and getting something out of them. One evening she was reading from *Martin Chuzzlewit*, the chapter where Alfred Jingle was commenting on the dangers of the stagecoach passing under too low an archway. "Children look around; Mother's head off— sandwich in hand and no mouth to put it in! Shocking! Shocking!" This struck Sis as being so irresistibly funny that she rolled on the floor, screaming with laughter, and kicked over the dollhouse in her exuberant glee.

The first house Dad built on his ranch was a one room log cabin with the customary dirt floor and roof, such as most settlers built on their newly acquired land, to establish residence. It was built on the north side of the North Fork the same side where the store and Swan Post Office could be reached without the necessity of fording the stream.

The first winter that Dad spent in his own homestead shanty, John Cluff spent on the ground he originally settled on, which was up on the flat below Elwood and had practically no water, and no shelter! One winter was enough for John, and when Dad urged him to "come down on the creek with me, there's room enough for both of us." John agreed.

Dad filed on his land as four forties in a square, and John, filed on his four forties in a row, saying he wanted all of that creek he could get! The two ranches were fenced as one and operated as one for many years. Cooperation was an essential, and these two young men who did not have much of anything (only "a wife and a couple of kids worth a million dollars of any man's money," as they used to express it), combined resources in every way.

Each had a saddle-horse, which was also "broke to harness;" as they took their few cattle out onto the open range in the spring and brought them in again in the fall. Jack and Joe were saddle horses, and good ones; then while the men were hauling poles to fence their ranches and build the needed corrals etc., Jack and Joe were a team, and a good one! Of course as time went by, Dad and John acquired more cattle and also more horses, but they often laughed together about the way they hauled their timber and put up their first crop of hay with just their two saddle horses.

When Dad and John Cluff built their houses on the adjoining ranches, in the late 1880s, on the other side

of North Fork, they built them exactly alike; three large rooms in an *ell* shape like this:
facing south so that the open area was sheltered from the westerly winds and was a very pleasant place for relaxing out-of-doors on summer evenings. The chief drawback to evenings outside was *mosquitoes*! We used to build a so-called smudge to discourage their attentions, this being a fire of chips, built in an old tin pan with green branches thrown on top to make it smoke. This could be moved around if the breeze varied, and was really pretty efficient at keeping the pests away. Timber was plentiful when these houses were built; the rooms were each fifteen by fifteen feet, and it was not difficult to get thirty-foot logs for such construction. The living room had a door and two full windows. Heat was furnished by wood stoves; one in the kitchen and one in the living room. Those log houses were really very warm and comfortable, even during Wyoming's cold winter weather.

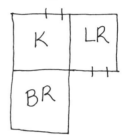

Dad had moved his old homestead cabin across the creek and laid it up again for a horse barn, built some adjoining hay-cribs and a corral, up the hillside a little way, by the boundary fence, which was known as the summer corral. This was used only during the summer season when both Dad's cows and John's were kept in the lower pasture, which was the lower end of John's ranch. In the evening, one of the Cluff boys and one of the Nichols girls would go after the cows, horseback. We took turns, Ez Cluff and my sister Lizzie one evening, and Chet and I the next evening. Normally it was a very simple procedure, but if there was any difficulty—strays in the herd, range bulls bothering, or something—Chet always came on up and corralled our cows himself. (Not of course, that I was a helpless little old gal! Anyway he never made me feel as though I were.) The cows were kept in overnight, milked in the morning, and then taken back to pasture. After the hay was harvested and the cows turned into the meadow, it was still a job for a kid from each family to get the cows in; but as soon as they were getting hay at night, the cows would come in themselves.

It was the custom among all the settlers, after the cattle were gathered in the fall, to go visiting to the homes of other ranchers and also to promote dances. It was on such occasions that the Cluff and Nichols women and children were bundled into the bed of the wagon-box, on a good layer of hay, with quilts spread over it. John and Dad mounted the spring-seat and away we went! I can remember going in that way to many a dance, at some ranch on Beaver Creek, Cow Creek, or the Encampment. It was the custom to go early, in order to arrive before dark, and then after an all-night feast and frolic, eat breakfast and come home by daylight. I can also remember a few occasions during "high-water" in the spring when we were returning from a dance, that the lower ford was such a torrent that water ran into the wagon-box, and dampened the women and children most uncomfortably. I was glad when Dad began insisting on the high-water ford, the place where the stream had broadened and ran into two channels.

Those old time country dances were much more than dances; just real get-togethers where people who had not seen each other for months could talk things over and compare notes. They would dance a while, visit a while, and probably nibble a snack or two before the big midnight supper. Any person with talent was called upon always; several of the men were buck-and-wing dancers or tap-dancers (my dad among the best). Some among both the men and the women could sing, and many were called on for readings. That was one of my dad's specialties and he was very popular with his rendition of "Ostler Joe," "Jim Bludsoe," and many others popular in those days—and most especially with the really *sad* ones. One lady used to say, "Hod, you'd draw tears from a turnip."—and he almost *would*—I could cry myself at this moment, just remembering how beautifully he spoke. But best of all I liked his singing; not necessarily at dances, but just all the time, around the house and at his work.

My sister too had a gift of music and Dad taught her to sing when she was only about three (Mother said) and as long ago as I can remember anything, I can see Dad calling Sis to him at some dance, setting her on his knee and saying, "Let's have 'Buffalo Gals,' huh?" and she would happily sing anything she was asked for. Anything that Dad sang, she learned with no apparent effort, and he certainly knew an amazing number of songs. No wonder people were impressed by that small girl having such a repertoire.

The musical instruments in evidence at most of the dances were violins. Elias Andrews, Pierce Culleton, and "Old Cush" (Medore Cushman) all had one. My dad had a flute and a five-stringed banjo which helped out on occasion. As my sister grew older, she played beautifully on both banjo and violin.

The lack of schools and churches presented problems to the early-day settlers. Mr. Wolfard, who was a qualified teacher, built a schoolhouse on his own ranch, and educated his own young family for a time. Later, after a schoolhouse was built across the river near the then "center of population," he was engaged to teach the public school—which he did for several terms. My mother was qualified to teach, but she felt that her attempts to teach my sister and me at home were not very satisfactory. The schoolhouse was a good four miles from our ranch but she decided to try letting us attend, the winter of 1891–2. My sister and I rode double on our gentle bay mare, Bess, and Dad arranged to have us leave her in the barn of Mr. William Platt, the current teacher, and walk on through the Peryam field the rest of the way. This was our first official attendance at school, when I was eight and my sister ten years of age. We both enjoyed it very much, in spite of the usual differences of opinion between sisters (and brothers, of course). We took turns riding in the saddle, while the other sat behind. When Sis rode in front, I grasped the tie-strings and hung on for dear life, for I knew as soon as we were out of sight of the house, Sis would let Bess run—and believe me she could run, nothing she liked better. We surely had some wild rides. Then when it was my turn to ride in front, and I did not like to ride fast, Sis would start kicking Bess in the ribs, and Bess would start kicking up behind; I could take my choice, let Bess go at least sort of fast or have her get madder and madder until she dumped us off. What a scaredy-cat I must have been! No wonder Sis got disgusted with me.

Our school career was a short one after all, as the weather soon got so cold and blizzardy the parents decided they had just better keep us at home. I remember Mr. Platt coming up to see us several times to help us with school work, and he was also anxious that we be in his special entertainment on the four-hundredth anniversary of Columbus's discovery of America. He had prepared a very elaborate program, and as Sis and I were both very good at memorizing, he did need us.

However, the weather got so very bad, we just could not be there, even for the entertainment. It was the following winter that our parents decided they would just have to take us to Colorado to go to school for a few years.

TORN AWAY FROM OUR HOME, JUST FOR THE MERE SAKE OF GOING TO SCHOOL, FORSOOTH!

IT WAS IN EARLY 1893, March I believe, that we left the dear old ranch. Dad sold his cattle for *twelve dollars a head* and nothing under a yearling counted. He left the ranch and his bunch of horses on the range in Uncle Ez's care, having sold his team and saddle horse. He said when we got back to the ranch again, he would break some more horses out of the wild bunch.

How we girls did cry! Mother and Dad had no idea, until the actual day of departure, how displaced Sis and I felt at being torn away from our home, just for the mere sake of going to school, forsooth! And so, even before we boarded the stage on the first lap of our journey, we were already looking forward to coming back.

The trip was rather trying. The stage route from Swan, by way of Saratoga, connected with the Union Pacific Railroad at Fort Fred Steele. The changing of stage horses, taking a meal at a road house, and the weariness of so many hours of stage travel are my chief remembrances. When we arrived at Fort Steele, Sis and I had our first view of a puffing, chuffing engine and its attendant train of cars.

We were met in Denver at an unseasonably early hour, by Grandpa, who was in the city on some political business or other, and who insisted on Dad attending a meeting with him that afternoon. Dad was anxious to get the family home to Boulder, but Grandpa would not take "no" for an answer. He saw that we had our breakfast and lunch, took us shopping where he bought Sis and me a nice pair of shoes each, and the most amazing amount of fruit, candy, and other treats to keep us happy at the hotel while Dad was attending the meeting. Mother was not a bit happy about the delay, but made the best of it. I don't think I ever spent a longer afternoon than that one; cooped up in a hotel room, for Mother simply refused to get out on the streets with us. We liked looking out of our upstairs window at the traffic, and I can see yet, Grandpa's bag of treats! It was a big, *big* paper bag, big as a hundred pound flour sack, filled with innumerable smaller bags of every kind of fruit, candy, or gum that Grandpa thought we might like! The hours certainly dragged. Watching traffic sort of palled after the first hour or so, and as Mother said, "After all, one can only eat so much!" She did however, let us stuff our little selves most amazingly, and for a wonder neither of us suffered any ill effects. Grandpa said, " I knew it wouldn't hurt 'em!"

We went on up to Boulder next day. Grandpa could not come. He was Lieutenant Governor of Colorado at that time, but Grandma and Aunt Franc met us at the depot with Old Doc (the family driving horse), and the surrey.

Brother Cliff was in school when we arrived, but I'll never forget my first glimpse of him! I had not seen him for three years, since he visited the ranch with Aunt Franc, and Grandma let me sit out on the front porch to watch for him. Sure enough, presently, here he came, swinging down the road, school-books in a strap slung over his shoulder—and such a long expanse of black stockings below his knee pants! I just couldn't wait for him to reach the house but ran to meet him crying "Cliff, Cliff!" at the top of my voice. He grinned all over his face, grabbed me by the shoulders and shook me, saying, "Snooks" and then swung me around to walk beside him, his arm around my shoulders, saying, "Wait till I change my clothes and we will go out under the evergreen and read the new *Youth's Companion.*" In a very few minutes he reappeared, dressed in his play-time jeans, with the *Youth's Companion* under his arm. He was eating an apple and had one for me, and we settled ourselves under the tree where he read to me. What a wonderful brother he always was!

Soon after we arrived in Boulder, Grandma, Grandpa and Aunt Franc went to Chicago to attend the World's Fair. We were living in their house while they were away and taking care of things for them. We three children were all in school, and looking forward to having Aunt Franc tell us about the fair when she returned. A little anecdote Aunt Franc told us afterward, when we were sitting on her bedroom floor and watching her unpack, stayed in our minds much longer, I think, than the "important" things she told us. Aunt Franc could always see a joke, even when it was on herself. It seems the relatives of Grandpa's—where they were staying while attending the fair—were quite wealthy people, owning a big fine farm with handsome buildings, and some of the finest horses in that part of the country. Aunt Franc visualized riding in the handsome carriage with a span of those high-stepping Kentucky thoroughbreds hitched to it. But it seemed the very first time they drove out, Uncle What's-His-Name had trouble catching the horse he wanted out in the pasture, and behold, he came in with a horse and a mule, which he hitched onto the handsome carriage, and away they went!

It was during that same summer of 1893 that Dad again went to work at the Colorado State Penitentiary; this time not as a guard, but as Yardmaster. He was third officer, the man in charge of prisoners. Home was the Prison Farm, which was leased by the Board of Directors of the Penitentiary and worked with convict labor. As the prisoners worked only in daylight hours, under a guard, the board offered Dad free use of the house if he cared to bring his family down, which of course he did. The farm was about a mile from the pen, on the eastern outskirts of Canyon City, and the house was pleasantly situated, and amply large, having three bedrooms, big pantry, full basement, and a large store-house across a closed porch from the kitchen, and of course the usual dining room and "parlor," as it was called in those days.

Mother liked the house, but I know she never grew accustomed to the prison laborers, "cons" as they were called, arriving every morning in the big wagons accompanied by armed guards, and to seeing them working the fields and orchards in their convict-stripe suits—and always the guard, very much in evidence, standing on the alert, with his rifle on his arm. Sis and I were never allowed to go away from the house during the hours the cons were there, but we did enjoy rambling over the big farm after they had been taken back to the pen for the night. Most of the time, it was just a small crew working, and only one guard, and they could all ride back to the pen in one big farm wagon. The guard who was in charge of this regular group, was an Irishman, named John Moran. I remember one evening during the apple season when Mr. Moran's crew had been picking and packing into barrels, he stopped the wagon by the house, after they were loaded in ready for the return trip, and came running up onto the porch where Dad was. His Irish eyes were twinkling and he said only, "Horace, look at their shirts!" as he turned and ran back to the wagon. Even my childish eyes could see that the would-be innocent faces of the cons were surmounted by much fatter bodies than usual. It was evident that nearly every man had one or more rows of apples around his midriff, under his carefully buttoned shirt. I don't see how Mr. Moran could keep a straight face and appear not to notice a thing. Must be an Irish gift.

It was during the fall months that Dad arranged with the authorities to keep one of the trustees on the farm day and night. He was paroled to Dad and was very, very grateful to be "on the outside" once more. Dad had a driving horse, and there was another old horse on the farm too. There was also a milk cow and chickens to care for, as well as a couple of pigs in a pen. It was the trustee's job to take care of them, and do any other work that Mother might want done.

He was really a very nice old man, and Dad always insisted he should never have been in the pen in the first place. It seems he got into a row with a neighbor over a line fence, and in some way laid himself liable to the law, and was committed to prison for a six-month term. He was with us until his term expired.

I'll never forget the evening before he was to leave us when Dad brought his suit of civilian clothes to him. He sat at the kitchen table holding the cheap coat in his lap, and rubbing his hand around the brim of the hat. There were tears in his eyes, and the expression of his face combined of shame, longing, and gratitude followed me through the years. In those days when an "ex-con" was practically an outcast, he was greatly ashamed of having served time—deserved or not—and very anxious to get home to his old wife, who had stuck to him through thick and thin. The fact that Dad had made it possible for him to spend most of his sentence on the farm was to him the greatest thing of all.

Next morning he came out to breakfast in his civilian clothes. When it was time to go, he gravely shook hands with us all, children included, saying, "Nichols, I can never thank you enough." He simply walked down the road and out of our lives. Never did he say a word to Dad about all the misery that Johnny, Mr. Moran's son, Sis, and I had dealt him in all the little ways mischievous children can conjure up. If either Dad or Mr. Moran had known about it they would have paddled us all until we couldn't sit down.

I cannot imagine what made us act so—just wanton mischief, as he was always unfailingly kind to us. We would put sandburs in the sweatband of his hat; we swiped the sunflower seeds he was drying on the bar roof and threw them into the river; we *jumped* on the big pumpkins he was saving to send to the fair, and when we found it locked, we tried everyway to get in (a whole orchard of fine apples free for our taking!) and finally Johnny managed to shove a big knot through a board on the back wall which left a hole big enough to get his hand through. He could get hold of an apple, but could not bring it back out through the hole, so he reached through the hole with his knife, and cut each apple he could reach into small enough pieces to bring out through the hole. What a sorry-looking mess of scrapped up apples we had before us! They did not look good enough to eat, so we just left them there. How the poor old trustee ever put up with us is more than I can see.

One day Dad came home and said to Mother, "Well, I'm out of a job. And I never *was* so damn happy."

"Goody," said Mother, "We'll go back up to Boulder," so we did. Just like that. I presume it was some sort of a political upheaval that lost him the job.

It was during that winter of 1893–4 that my very active sister slipped on an icy doorstep and fell, wrenching her hip very badly. This was the beginning of a long and trying time for her. Hip-joint disease, as it was then called, set in, and she had a long bout with sciatic rheumatism. Our old family physician, Dr. Allen, did everything for her that was possible but he said as such a big overgrown child, she had outgrown her strength, and it was long months before she was able to get around the house a little, even with the aid of crutches. Later she was fitted with a steel brace, to keep the inflamed ball-joint out of its socket to a certain extent. This brace she wore for many years, and even after she had been allowed to discard it, she still used crutches.

Those early months of her illness were a sad time for us all. There seemed so little we could do to ease or comfort her. She liked to play the banjo and would lie for hours, propped up on her pillows picking out new tunes. Brother Cliff used to come over nearly every day after school and they would both play.

I brought home a big blue Maltese cat for her one day; it had insisted on staying at the schoolhouse where he definitely was *not* welcome, and I knew she would love him. She did. She called him "Sancho" and he was full of tricks and whimseys. Having been an alley cat for so long he had no sense of discipline, and would steal any food he could find, even though he had a plateful before him. Dad said he must have been hungry for so long he didn't intend to take chances on a famine. One day though, he really overdid it. Sis was sitting by the stove, watching Mother fry the dinner sausages, and had Sancho in her lap. The sausages were popping and bubbling and smelling most appetizing, and Sancho kept licking his chops and looking at them until finally he jumped up and hopped right on top of the stove, evidently intending to grab one; however, his blistered toes caused him to jump down at once! When I got home from school, Sis had him in her lap and his poor blistered toes wrapped in cloths with sweet-oil. The feet healed up pretty promptly but Sancho kept off stoves after that.

Sancho used to beg for everything he saw us eating and Sis used to like to make sugar taffy. The first time he begged while we were pulling taffy, Sis told him, "Oh, you wouldn't like this." But he kept on, so finally she gave him some. He bit down on the sticky lump and stuck his jaws together. He tried clawing at his mouth, but finally gave it up, sat down, and wrapped his tail around his toes and purred—as if he was very happy— until finally it all melted away enough so he could get his mouth open. Then he promptly yowled for more. Ever after, when we made taffy it was part of the fun to see Sancho clamp his jaws shut and then purr delightedly until he finally got the best of the bit of taffy.

Dr. Allen, who was not only the family physician, but a warm personal friend brought Sis a white rat, with pink eyes, complete with a bird cage. She was pleased and named it "Tatty." The next morning when Mother got up, she saw a small reddish object about the size of the first joint of her thumb, lying on the floor. Pretty soon she saw another, and then she kept on seeing them—baby rats, who were small enough to wriggle through the bars of the bird cage. How Sis did laugh! Eleven, I believe that was the first family. They were the cutest little rascals while they were growing to full size, and they cheered many an hour for her. However, *rats* soon became superfluous, and were given to anyone who would accept one or more, but Sis always kept Tatty and cherished her until Tatty died.

After Sis got able to get around a little, it became an established custom for either Cliff or Grandpa to take her for a drive in the phaeton every afternoon. Then some relative of Mother's died and left her a little money and she and Dad decided to buy a gentle horse and buggy so Sis could drive out at any time without inconveniencing anyone. The search for the proper kind of horse began, and at last he was found. Prince, a beautiful all-white horse with a pink nose, was kind, intelligent and, above all, gentle. Just right for Sis, and he was one of the family for many years. It soon became evident that the time spent out in the open air was helping Sis regain her strength, and seldom a day went by without a drive, long or short. Sometimes she was out practically all day. On Saturdays and Sundays, I went with her. Many a happy drive we had, up Boulder Canyon, or Sunshine Canyon, or perhaps "around the horn" as we called it, down by Valmont, around by Weisenhorn's Lake and then home. They were happy days, jogging along behind the fat white pony.

He was so snow white, it was quite a problem keeping him clean. He had a habit, as soon as he was unhitched and turned into the pasture, of rolling in a dust pile—or even a mud-puddle, if one was available. Then what a scouring he had to have with the currycomb and brush if we wanted to drive him again. He was broken to saddle too, and although I had no saddle I sometimes used to ride him bareback, down to meet Dad as he was coming home from work.

At that difficult period in our lives, Dad was Road Supervisor—hard and heavy work but he was glad to have it. Joe Latorra was his helper. During the winter of 1878–9 Grandfather had brought home Joe, a refugee Italian boy, who had lost an eye. When Joe first came he could speak no English at all. He had a sunny disposition and was very grateful to Grandfather. Later Joe lived with the family of his brother Frank, who lived within a block of our home. Dad used to say that Joe did more than his share toward caring for Frank's large and ever-growing family. Joe was just heartsick over Sis's illness and crippled condition, and was always doing little things for her in the way of small surprises. Seldom a day passed but he came to see her—or at least he would wave his black hat as he passed her window and sing, "Howa da girl?" She always looked forward to seeing Joe. He loved music and liked to hear her play or sing. One evening she was singing a hymn and he asked her, "You knoa 'We're a marchi in the beautiful light of God?' I singa da chorus." He did, and a very good voice he had. That song became a part of Sis's repertoire from that time forward. "Joe's Song," we always called it, saying "march i" as he did, for *ing* was too much for Joe's Italian tongue.

During the year 1896, a healer appeared in Denver and performed some miraculous cures, making headline news for weeks. Joe did his best to get Dad to take Lizzie to the healer. He knew she would be instantly healed, but Dad would not. Later, the papers began to tell about the healer blessing various objects—handkerchiefs, and the like—which were the property of people who could not come to him. These objects, which were personally blessed by the healer and then returned to their owners, helped many. So Joe came over to get one of Sis's handkerchiefs and made a special trip to Denver to have it blessed for her. When he brought it back, he showed her how the healer said to hold it tightly in the closed hand, and feel the healing power spreading through the entire body. I feel if Sis could have *believed* as earnestly as Joe did in the healing power of that handkerchief, the cure would certainly have been effected.

It was Christmas time, that year of 1896, that Sis's special wish was for a violin of her own. Joe came to Dad and said, "You no getta da fid for Liz? I *getta!*" Dad assured him that he and Mother were planning to get the violin, so he said, "Good, good," flashed one of his beaming smiles, and went away.

Sis always liked to get him to talk about his boyhood days in Italy; he described things so vividly we almost felt as though we had actually seen them. Lizzie particularly was pleased to hear about the "hills all covered with grape vines," as she was very fond of grapes, and such vineyards as he described were almost more than she could imagine. Over and over she would ask him to tell about them, which he would do, adding some new little detail each time until it was almost like a fairy tale to her. That Christmas time, he brought her a brooch, a *perfect* bunch of grapes, about two and one-half inches long, with the proper brown stem and green leaf. It was really exquisite.

That was the last Christmas we spent in Boulder. My heart's desire that year was for a baby doll, nothing else mattered at all—just as Cliff's heart was set on the banjo and Lizzie's on the fiddle. The grandparents, parents, aunt, and (Uncle) Joe Latorra quizzed us all through the fall trying to find out what we most wanted, and we gave them all sorts of wild answers. Cliff told them he wanted a krokinole board and a bicycle, while I (graceless cub) when my dear Grandmother

asked what sort of musical instrument I preferred—
she had found out Sis and Cliff each wanted one—I
thought of her flower gardening (which I admired) and
told her, "I guess a rake or hoe will be about right for
me." Then I saw she was really in earnest and I told her
I wanted a mandolin! God knows I had neither use nor
desire for such. Kids are funny. It was my grandmother, just the same, who found it was the baby doll I wanted.

We had the Christmas tree over at Grandma's in
the pompous red plush parlor that we used only on special occasions. The parlor had an ornate big heater with
an iron horse on top of it, the like of which I had never
seen, before or since. Grandpa, Grandma, Aunt Franc,
Cliff, Dad, Mother, Sis, and I were all cozily grouped
around the room, eating candy, nuts, and popcorn all
over Grandma's red velvet carpet—with never a cross
look cast at us. My memories of that Christmas Eve
focus on my brother Cliff, with his banjo and his shin-
ing eyes, and me and my doll. We always gravitated
into a corner together, so there I sat on that hard mon-
strosity of a red plush sofa and him on a footstool in
front of me. Playing his soft plinkety-plunk to me, the
grownups conversation went on over our heads and
beyond our ears. I finally had to be detached from that
corner to go home, and Cliff still had his banjo in his
hands when they came to the door to wish us good-
night.

They had dinner with us the next day, and Cliff and
Sis did some violin and banjo playing together. Of
course I got asked what I was going to call the doll, and
finally my crusty old Granddad (probably disgusted
with all the twaddle) said, "Call her Dorcas!" Well, I
loved my grandpop and somebody else suggested
"Helena" (though why I don't know), so I said I guessed

I'd call her Helena Dorcas, but I felt very damp and crushed. Later my own good mother got me convinced that Grandfather was only joking and wanted me to name her my own self, whatever I liked. So I named her Elizabeth Isabel after my grandma and because Isabel was my favorite name. After the festivities, Grandma asked if she might borrow my doll for a little while. Well, I could hardly spare the doll—but if *Grandma* wanted her, of course I said, "Yes." Grandma said she would send her home by Cliff after a while, unless I would let her stay all night. Would I? Again I said yes, and when my doll came back to me, Grandma had knitted her a beautiful pair of red stockings. [The Christmas of 1896 as described in a letter to Vera Oldman, November 21, 1942]

MY HOW GOOD THE DEAR OLD RANCH DID LOOK TO US THAT DAY, AFTER FOUR LONG YEARS AWAY FROM IT

I WAS HAVING SUCH A HARD TIME in school that winter, I do not remember hearing much of the family planning about our return to Wyoming in the spring. All of us, and Sis in particular, were very eager to get back home to the ranch! Dr. Allen said he saw no reason why the overland trip would be any hardship on Sis, it might instead be looked upon as beneficial. As the plans gradually worked out, Sis was to have a spring cot so she would be in no danger of damp ground under her bed. We had a good wall tent, large enough to "sleep" us. Day travel for the family would be in a small covered wagon, drawn by our Prince and another gentle horse—which Dad would buy for the purpose of getting us to Wyoming, then sell after we were safely home. He had to buy also a work-team and heavy wagon to transport our furniture and other goods; he would arrange to have a neighbor who wished to go to Wyoming take his own team and heavy wagon for the trip. All these plans sounded very glamorous to me and I could hardly wait for the time to come.

Dad wanted to start the first of May, to get ahead of the high water in the rivers we would need to cross. Gradually the equipment needed began to accumulate.

The horse he found to drive with Prince was white, or rather a flea-bitten gray. He was not pretty like Prince, but rawboned and angular. He had one foot that been injured, just above the hoof, by being caught between two logs at a sawmill. The foot had healed up, but was enlarged and did not add to his appearance. He was called Jim, and he so endeared himself to us during our

Studio Portrait
Horace Nichols in 1893
This photograph was taken in Canyon City, Colorado, where he worked as a guard at the penitentiary.

difficult trip north that Mother wept when he was sold, and said, "I hope they *appreciate* Jim." He was an old horse but kind and faithful, and always willing to do his best. As Dad expressed it, "A better horse never looked through a collar." The team Dad bought, expecting to keep them for work on the ranch, were much

Studio Portrait

Sylvia Wilson Nichols in 1901

larger than Prince and Jim—about 1,400 pounds and were called Duke and Kate.

Dad engaged the services of a young man named Robbins to drive the team on the trip north. Mr. Robbins being more than happy to make the trip, if he could lead his saddle pony behind the wagon, so he would have a means of transportation back to Boulder. He was a young chap, about twenty years old and full of enthusiasm, but quite inexperienced in handling horses. The other man to join us, using his own team and wagon to transport our goods, was Mr. Burke. Dad had arranged to rent the house (as of May 1) to an elderly couple, M. and Mrs. Smith, who were neighbors.

I, like the rest of my classmates in school, had just started to keep a diary.

April 26, 1897. It was a lovely day, warm and pleasant. Papa had work in court every day since the Monday before Easter. I washed my head with Packer's tar soap for the second time this evening. Our willow is nearly leafed out. We have to be out of our house next Monday so Mr. Smith can have it. Papa is going to set up the tent for us to live in until we go up north. The tent is ten by fourteen. Last Friday I had my teeth fixed and Sunday I went up Boulder Canyon with Ada and then she came down with me. Mamma washed today and we were through by noon. Last week Papa put in eleven shifts, six days and five nights at court. He came home tonight.

April 27, 1897. Lizzie found some violets today, and it rained in the afternoon and evening. Lizzie and I packed our doll trunks and I cleaned my stand and packed my work-box today. Mamma packed the fruit in the brown box. Papa came home tonight. We

ironed today. I read "Agatha's History." Ralph Davis
bought eggs of us. Lora

April 30, 1897. Joe and Frank Latorra brought our
tent and wagon-cover, old Duke is nearly white now
but he looked pretty red in the rain. (Today) Papa
did not come from town until three o'clock this
morning but he got up and set our tent up for us.
Mamma and I packed considerably today. I took out
the tacks from the sitting-room carpet and Lizzie
took most of the tacks in our bedroom carpet and
Mamma's bedroom is the only one in the house that
has a carpet. We took four chairs and a small table
out in the tent and my room looks as bare as can
be—it has only Lizzie's stand and my bed in it. Mr.
Smith brought a load of coal today. I moved Spot's
kittens into tent. Lora Nichols

At this very inconvenient time old man Jupiter
Pluvius let down a twelve-inch fall of snow. What con-
sternation when we got up that morning, realizing our
trip just had to be postponed. Dad shoveled paths to
the barn, and coal-shed and as the chickens were let
out, these paths were the only places they could travel.
Prince was, as usual, very much in evidence and he
grew exasperated with these hens underfoot and started boosting them along with his nose. One frightened
hen, unused to such treatment, tried to escape by flying
up one of the banks beside the path, but stuck in the
soft snow and hung there, perfectly helpless. Prince
laid back his ears and angrily bit at her. He caught her
by the back and shook her as a dog might have done
until she stopped moving and then dropped her. Of
course the poor thing was dead and we ate her for our
dinner that day, and Mr. Prince lost his liberty and
remained tied up in the barn every day until the snow
had melted.

Studio Portrait
Lizzie and Lora in 1897
The photograph was taken in Boulder, before the family's return
to Wyoming

So much moisture had fallen that Dad said it would
be ten days before the roads would be dry enough to
start north. An added complication was that he would
not dare start later than that or the streams would be
too high to ford. We camped right there on our own
place until the tenth, when we made our start.

*May 4, 1897. We slept in the tent last night. Papa left
his clothes on all but his shoes and stockings but the
rest of us undressed. We slept very well and all feel
well today. Lizzie and I went up town with the
buggy this morning. Papa preceded us on foot and
while Lizzie was in a store I saw him. His gypsy-
bows have not come. This afternoon he has been fix-*

*ing the cover to his little wagon. I like it very much
to camp out.*

*May 7, 1897. We sat around the campfire so long
that we slept late this morning and Peter caught us
in bed. I went to Mrs. Cotton's this morning. Lizzie
and I sat for pictures. We got a picture of quartet.
Papa got a gun. Old Duke has a mustache. Aunt
Sallie gave me a California potpourri, blue. Went
over to Grandma's with Papa and he traded hay-
rake for spring-seat. Papa took Duke and Kate to be
shod. Kate is buckskin. Duke is almost white. I am
to give Aunt Sallie stories. Had Lizzie's medicine
prescriptions written.*

Lora W. N
i
c
h
o
l
s

I am to make cartridge belt.

Cliff came over to say good-bye the evening before
we were to start, and we sat around the campfire and
visited. Grandma had tried, when Dad first decided to
go, to get me to say I would stay with her and go to
school, but as much as I hated leaving Cliff, all I could
say was, "But I've got to go with Dad." The next morning when we were loaded up and ready to start, we
drove around in front of Grandma's house; nobody
came out. Mother went around to the east door of the
kitchen, and then on through the west door, and out to
the wash-house. In a few minutes she came out with
her handkerchief in her hand and her eyes suspicious-
ly moist. "Go in and say good-bye, Horace, they are not

coming out." Dad climbed down over the wagon wheel, cocked his hat over his eyes, and started down the walk. I couldn't stand seeing Dad look like that, so I climbed out too and ran and took his hand. We went out to the wash house, where we found Grandma and Aunt Franc getting weekly laundry underway. Grandma kissed me, patted me, and said, "my *good* girl," and turned me over to Aunt Franc who was crying. I was so distressed to see Aunt Franc in tears that I was hugging her and trying to get her to stop crying so that I really did not hear what Dad and Grandma were saying, until Dad turned and said in an awful voice, "Franc! Why didn't you *tell* me how she felt?"

"She wouldn't let me, brother."

Dad turned back to his mother and said, "Why, I'll turn the damn wagons back, and stay!"

"No, Horace, Sylph wouldn't be happy." It was at this point that Dad gave a mighty sob and we started back to the wagon, hand in hand. So we had a rather sad start.

May 10, noon. Started about 8.30. Just camped this side of Longmont. Grandma's Good bye. We ate our dinner in true camp style. There is no water where we camp that is fit to drink. Lots of fun. We went on through Longmont and Papa bought two collar-pads. We began looking for a camping place about six o'clock. We had no hay so we looked out for farmers with hay stacks. We had just crossed the Little Tompson and wanted to camp. There were two houses upon the hill and Joe went up to see if we could buy some hay, but they had none to spare so we went on. About two miles further we found a place and got some hay and some fine water.

Dad had tried hard to get Joe Latorra to make the trip with us, but Joe felt that he was needed too badly at home (which he certainly was, as Dad could see) but he promised to go one day's journey with us, until Dad could get his two new men sort of acquainted with the routine of such a journey. Joe would ride with us for a while, then jump down and run ahead to the next wagon which Mr. Robbins was in charge of. Sometimes he would drive a ways for Mr. Robbins or "Robber" as he persisted in calling him. Mr. Robbins told Dad later he showed him a lot about how to handle the horses, without appearing to be coaching him at all. He did not spend so much time on the lead wagon with Mr. Burke. Joe would wave his hands, flash a grin, and say to Dad, "Burke, he know it all." At our noon camp, Joe showed Mr. Robbins a better way to tie his pony behind the wagon. The pony was afraid of that high swaying wagon-box in front of him, and kept pulling back and breaking his halter rope. Joe got a heavier rope, put it around his neck, and knotted it into his halter ring as well.

May 11, 1897. It rained this morning. We camped this side of Berthoud last night. They call it six miles from Berthoud to Loveland, but everyone Papa asked (and we) thought it was the longest six miles ever traveled. We camped about two miles from Loveland for dinner. We started at 8.40 this morning and went through Loveland at eleven o'clock. We went through Fort Collins and nearly to LaPorte this afternoon. Cache La Poudre is the name of the creek we have just crossed. We camped just the other side of above. Lovely place.

We certainly felt gloomy next morning when we were all loaded up ready to start, and Joe walked off down the railroad track to take the train back to Boulder. Even Mr. Burke and Mr. Robbins had learned to appreciate Joe during those two days of adjustment period. Our noon camp was by the Forks Hotel that day, and our night camp at Deadman. Dad had said the folks at the Forks Hotel used to keep Angora goats and if they still had them, he would get me one. I was quite disappointed to find they no longer had them, but I don't doubt Mother was relieved.

It was the next day, May 13, that we reached Tie Siding. We got there about noon as I had an upset stomach—Mother thought from the continual jolting of the wagon—we stayed there until three in the afternoon. We made an early night camp at the north end of Boulder Ridge, where there was plenty of wood and good feed for the horses. Dad was quite concerned about various bad reports he had received about the road ahead.

Next day, the fourteenth we made it to Mountain Home, and from there on, our troubles were many. The roads were quite muddy, and the next day, May 15, we got stuck for the first time. We made our noon camp at Pinkham. About two miles beyond there, Mr. Burke's team got swamped and Dad had to hook Duke and Kate onto his load to pull it out. One of Mr. Burke's horses had a tendency to balk, and he wouldn't try to fight them through the mud hole for that reason.

That night we camped at the Laramie River. It was not fordable, and the bridge was not fixed yet—although they were working on it. Dad had already sent Mr. Robbins on his pony over the old Hunter ranch to see if we could ford there, but word came back it was not fordable. It was a muddy and uncomfortable camp that night, and more rain fell. Next morning the workmen managed to get the floor of the bridge in sufficiently good repair so that we could cross over. We made it nearly to Pearl that night, after getting stuck and very nearly balking old Duke. The roads were practically bottomless. The night before, Duke got loose and into the oats, eating nearly 100 pounds of them, and could not have water all day. As Dad said, "No wonder he balked."

The next morning, May 17, we went about three miles and got badly stuck. Dad had to take the big team and pull Mr. Burke's load out, and then Duke and Kate couldn't pull their own load, which was heavier. The final straw that broke the camel's back was the pony, tied behind; that swaying load ahead and mud splashing all around caused him to set his feet and literally *slide*. That added burden at the crucial moment is what stuck Duke and Kate; after that they wouldn't try for a while. Mr. Robbins untied the pony and I led him up the road ahead, out of the way. Mr. Robbins tried to tell Dad he was gentle and I could ride him, but Dad was afraid to have me try it. The pony seemed so wild-eyed when Mr. Robbins rode him, so I led the pony on up the mountain, letting him graze along the side of the road as I watched the men struggle with the mired wagon. Dad finally unhooked Prince and Jim from the family wagon and put them ahead of Duke and Kate. None of them were in the habit of working as a four-horse team, and they were all excited anyway, so it was some time before Dad could get them to pull *together*. It was good old Jim who saved the day. He kept utterly calm through it all and obeyed every order Dad gave him. It was a sight to see that one small, old, gray steed acting as though he could move the whole thing alone! Some of the mud holes just seemed to have no bottom and the trees were so thick we could not go around them. We camped only about six miles farther than our previous night's camp.

We got an early start and made it nearly to Collins that day, camping on the Little Beaver Creek. As soon as we broke camp and got on the road, Sis and I began to sing all the Civil War songs and a lot of others, occasionally interrupting ourselves to point out a landmark as soon as we could see the Encampment valley. Next day, May 19, we reached Uncle Ez's at 2.30, where we were heartily welcomed and well fed. We stayed overnight and went to the ranch the next morning. We were somewhat worried about how high the water would be in North Fork, but Dad said he didn't think it would be too bad.

It seemed to us that many changes had occurred during our four years absence. Of course, we knew that Uncle Guy Nichols had died while we were in Boulder, but we found it hard to realize. The Swan Post Office and store were closed, and a grocery had been opened at Riverside (then called "Doggett") by Johnson Doggett and his brother, Newton. Newt was in charge of the store, which was in a tent at that time.

We not only had the town of Doggett, but an eastern syndicate had established a town called Grand Encampment City, on the windswept hill between Doggett and Dad's ranch. It seems the townsite company had wanted to build their town at Doggett, but were unable to agree with H.P. (Doc) Culleton on a price for the land. This was Doc's homestead, and when he would not agree to sell for what they considered a fair price, they just did the next best thing.

That twentieth of May, 1897, when we drove up over the Riverside hill and saw the embryo town Dad said, "Well, there goes my homestead!" It had been his intention to file on the part of the townsite adjoining

"The Dear Old Ranch"

his ranch as a homestead. But that sunny morning, a line was being plowed around the townsite, and one log cabin and a few tents made a brave showing, with the Stars and Stripes flying over the company office.

We came through the regular ford, below the old Cluff place (by then owned by Dell Fleming), and while the water reached the wagon box, it did not run in. My, how good the dear old ranch did look to us that day, after four long years away from it! The twentieth of May has been a red-letter day in our family ever since, as the day we got home.

That first week, we were pretty busy getting settled, and of course we did have some company. Uncle Platt Hinman, Aunt Nan, and cousin Carrie came up from Saratoga, and one day Uncle Ez's family came to dinner.

The day after we arrived, Mr. Burke and Mr. Robbins started out to go and visit Saratoga. They were driving in Mr. Burke's wagon, and Mr. Robbins had the pony tied behind so he could ride back, as Mr. Burke expected to head right back to Boulder. As I was watching them ride down the road, they met Gene Fleming, who brought Mr. Robbins a letter. Mr. Robbins hopped out of the wagon, got on the pony bareback, and guided him by the halter. As he rode into the yard where Dad and I were standing, he said, "That letter is from my mother. I'll have to take the train right back to Boulder." Sliding off the pony he said to me, "Would you like to have the pony?" When I managed to gasp "Yes," he said, as he handed me the halter rope, "He's all yours."

I looked at dad who nodded his consent and said, "Take off his halter, Snooks, and turn him loose in the pasture. He'll be all right." So I did, and I'm sure no millionaire ever had the world and everything that's in it to such an extent as I had, when I watched that pony trot down the road and join our other horses.

Mr. Robbins called him "Nibbs." He told me the horse's name was really "His Royal Nibbs," but he just called him "Nibbs" for short. So Nibbs he remained. Dad wasn't very happy about it, and that evening wanted to know if I wouldn't like to trade Nibbs for one of Gene Fleming's pintos. I thought the pintos were pretty cute and I knew they were gentle, but I told Dad I'd rather keep Nibbs. So he said all right—that I could keep him. I was so excited over it that I could hardly sleep that night. I know I must have started looking wistful at Dad as soon as I sat down to my breakfast for he said, "We'll try him out after breakfast."

He saddled Prince, and then put my side-saddle on Nibbs, and the bridle that Mr. Robbins said he always used because Nibbs had a hard mouth. It was a double bar bit; then he attached a leading rein to the ring in one side of my bridle. After helping me into the saddle (and seeing that I had the reins properly held) he kept the leading rein in his hand as he mounted Prince. We started down the road, very sedately, side by side. We hadn't gone fifty feet when Dad gave a quizzical smile, reached over, and unsnapped the leading rein from my bit, and said, "Well, Robbins told the truth, he is perfectly gentle. You can ride him anytime you want to." He left us, all on our own—which did not disturb the pony a bit. I rode around the pasture for a while and tried out his paces, as Dad had told me to do. We trotted and galloped, and finally settled on an easy canter that was just right for a side-saddle. Then I rode up to the house to show him to Mother. She was waiting to rejoice with me over my good fortune—just as she always was, God bless her. To an unprejudiced observer, Nibbs would no doubt have seemed "just an Indian cayuse." To me, however, he was the most remarkable horse in the world—and my very own.

Part II

An Edited Collage of Lora's Work

I INTEND ALWAYS TO KEEP A DIARY

DURING THE EARLY YEARS following the Nichols' return to the homestead in 1897, finding paper was one of Lora's foremost problems; in solving this shortage, she was creative and persevering.

> *Sat. Feb. 5, 1898. Papa got some bacon & it had around it some funny blue-green sort of paper. I am going to make into Diarys. I have cut out those green leaves & I have 18 colored leaves enough for 6 more books like Diary No. 6. The folks are all in bed. I would like to sit up and make Diaries but I'd better not.*

> *Mon. Feb. 21, 1898. Lizzie spoilt her pink table cover so I have got some more pink paper for Diaries all I lack now is white. I have pink, blue & yellow but no white. Anyway I have got 10 Diaries made.*

Living in the Victorian Age, albeit on an isolated homestead in Wyoming, young Lora was concerned about the state of her character and also of her soul. With more than a touch of adolescent dramatics, she often viewed herself as one of the lost, a hopeless rebel. Diary recorded not only those instances when she perceived she had fallen from grace, but also her resolutions for improvement.

Wed., Dec. 22, 1897. I am going to try to not be such a selfish beast... Mamma expects to clean tomorrow. I hope I shall stick to my resolution long enough to help her.

Sun., Mar. 27, 1898. I was to have started yesterday to read the Bible 3 chaps. week days & 5 Sundays. Will mark arrears on back cover.

Wed. Apr. 13, 1898. I am going to read 5 chapters weekdays & 10 on Sundays after this.

Sun. Apr. 15, 1898. I am a liar!! I am a L-I-A-R. LIAR, liar. Liar. Liar.

Taking inspiration and condemnation from her reading, Lora especially felt herself incapable of reaching the perfection of the unsullied heroines of her favorite novels.

Wed., Dec. 22, 1897. I want to be like Jennie Burton in "A Face Illumined."

Sat., Jan. 15, 1898. I was reading in "Jack & Jill" how Merry missionaried and I went straight and cleaned up my room & tidied it .

Lora's diaries contain innumerable poems, sayings, and excerpts from longer works which were to guide her improvement.

Wed. July 6, 1898. I read somewhere a long while ago that "One cannot change one's nature; only help to develope [sic] the good and control the bad," and it has been "sticking in my craw" ever since. I don't know where it was I read it but I think it was in one of Louisa Alcott's books.

However, proving that Lora could have a literary model, if not a moral one, in the notorious, fictitious juvenile of the time, she commented:

Wed. June 8, 1898. I wish I could write a good diary like the bad boy.

It was natural that Lora should seek literary models for her writing as well as her character. Reading aloud had been a family tradition for the Nichols family since the early days at Swan, when they lived in Uncle Guy's dirt-floored shanty. Dickens was always a favorite.

Fri. Mar. 11, 1898. We started to read Little Dorrit aloud.

Reading alone, Lora became omnivorous; on January 4, 1898, she noted, "I am going to take a resolution now not to read but one book a month. I read more than is good for me." She never mentioned being disenchanted or discouraged with any of her reading which included such titles as Carlyle's *History of the French Revolution* and Reade's *Very Hard Cash*; she copied in her diary favorite lines from all works, including Reade's.

Sat. Jan. 14, 1899. Dr. Sampson is always making little rhymes and one of them is:

He had the luck to be a male
So like a rat without a tail
Could do, could do, could do.

What books and magazines came her way were generally making their rounds among relatives and friends.

Sat. May 14, 1898. [Cousin] Carrie & I went to Uncle Ez's on Billy & Nibbs & got "Bad Boy's Diary," "Tom Sawyer," "Huckleberry Finn" & "Robinson Crusoe."

Mon. June 13, 1898. I am going to take up for Aunt Nannie a can of milk, a pound of butter my two new books (Reb & his friends & Brace Bridge Hall) the new McClure's magazine, Cliff's letter and all of the latest newspapers.

The following year the boom town just a mile from the homestead produced its first newspaper. *The Grand Encampment Herald* would one day provide Lora with the strand of early town history to be woven with the accounts from the diary to create her memoir, *I Remember.*

...the *Grand Encampment Herald* started publication. Owned by the Herald Publishing Co., it was edited and printed by Ed Drury and his brother Will. It was a big day in town when the old Washington hand press started printing that first edition dated Mar 18 1899; everybody standing around "Bidding" for the first copy to come off the press, which finally went to Hank Ashley for ten dollars

(IR, 57).

MAMMA WASHED

HAVING A ROOM not only afforded Lora her own sleeping space, but also a private space to pursue her two favorite introspective pastimes, confiding in her diary and reading. Soon after the family's return, Papa made changes in the house he had built on North Fork; "Our rooms are progressing. He has nearly finished plastering in my room. They are very nice" (Saturday, Nov. 20, 1897). Although Lora remembered with pleasure the one-room shanty at Swan, with its dirt floor covered with hides, she reveled in her "dear den" at the ranch.

Friday early in the morning Nov. 26. All the upper sash of my window has beautiful frost pictures. So have the two lower panes of the other but the two upper panes have only a row of trees so one can see out. The snow is drifted some and packed & frozen. It is blowing a little now....

Tue. Dec. 21, 1897. ...My room is a dear den all my very own. Lying on one side in bed as I usually do I look at my door. On one side is a nice picture, a great friend of mine; it is an advertisement of Midland coffee but that does not hurt it any. It is a lovely large Newfoundland dog in a room and a little tot of

*a girl standing on tip toe just laying a grain of coffee
on his nose. She has a package of coffee held with
one arm, from which a few grains have fallen and
are lying on the carpet. The little girl has a sweet
face with blue eyes and golden hair. It is a very pretty picture. On the other side of my door hangs my
banjo for which I have the very limited Repertoire of
twenty tunes but I am learning more. Here too,
directly under my banjo are two picture cards. One
is of a large pink rose in a bouquet of white flowers
and green leaves. It was sent to me years ago when I
was a small child by a favorite aunt of mine. I have
had it almost twelve years now. When I was small I
used to think that was the most beautiful card that
was ever made I still think a great deal of it, however. The other is of a pretty little girl dancing in a
path with grass on each side and two white tame
rabbits dancing in front of her....*

*Tue. Jan 18, 1898. ...I have soda-pop materials in
my room mixed up & my room locked. My Birdy is
in here now (night) & I covered his cage with Bells
quilt to keep him warm....*

*Wed. Jan 19, 1898. I moved Birdy out in the front
room again as it is too cold in here. I enjoyed a dish
of snow cream & one of "pop."...I am going to....
undress and put on my bloomers & be a boy awhile
and drink a glass of soda pop—I have them on now
and have drunk my soda pop. When I was putting
them on, my curtain suddenly shot up & I nearly
jumped out of my skin.*

*Mon. June 6, 1898. ...I cleaned my room today too
but not as thoroughly as Libsey did. I swept the
floors ("under the beds" and all) and picked up all of
our doll traps and put them in some sort of order.
Charlie's old overcoat is on the floor now and a bit*

of a fingerstall on a chair, my doll box littered with
work basket, pattern box, Scissors, sewing and bits
of cloth and thread so you can see how clean I am.
There is a mustard can, curling iron and paper,
empty ink bottle, bucksaw handle, Birdy's bathing
dish, a nail and several pieces of cuttlebone on my
plant shelves not to mention 'the cards' Birdy has
left when he called there. I will have to clean them
tomorrow. Don't you think they need it?

Lora's freedom in having her own den—where she could place on her walls whatever she wished, decide whether to clean or not to clean, or to lounge surreptitiously in her bloomers and drink soda pop—undoubtedly was rare among settler's children. She recorded a night spent with the neighbors, the Flemings and the Herrings, in an overflowing house.

+Tue. Oct. 24, 1899. Yesterday Mum had the tooth-
ache again. Pop went to Lordier and got some medi-
cine but it didn't help it much and when we had
eaten dinner Pop took her down to Cloud City
[Grand Encampment] to see if they could get it
pulled. I washed up the dishes, and sat around until
five, went and got the cows and then as they hadn't
got back I went to work getting supper. When I had it
nearly ready, George Herring came up and told me
that Pop and Mum had gone to Toga because they
couldn't get it pulled here. He told Mum that he
would see that I was "cared for" (Lord!) and that the
chores were done. He said for me to go home with
him to stay all night...I slept with Lindy and Job.
The boys slept in a bed beside us. Once I waked up
with Job punching me in the back and Lindy's fist
under my head and Gary (who had come and
crawled in at the foot) occupying the place rightly
belonging to my nether limbs, a little corner of quilt

*over my "middle" and my nightgown around my
neck. I had a great deal of trouble disposing of my
feet until I hit upon the happy plan of putting them
under Gary's pillow and then comfortably balanced
on the thin edge of nothing, I dropped peacefully off
to sleep. It reminded me of Washington's sleeping 5
in bed (when he slept with his fore fathers you
know). It is snowing Billy Guns and I don't know
whether Pop and Mum will come home or not. 8.15
P.M. They got here O.K. Pop got her the swellest pair
of shoes. O me! O my! Sears (the dentist) pulled her
tooth.*

In the house Lora and Lizzie assisted Mamma with
the myriad chores. "Mamma washed" were the most
frequent words Lora penned into Diary. Mamma
washed with the board and the stomper and the tub.
The clothes and linens were starched stiff and ironed
with the flat iron. Lora slipped almost imperceptibly
from making doll clothes at age fifteen to making her
own the following year, assuming that chore from her
mother. The women of the household cleaned all the
usuals plus wooden floors, chimneys and lamps, coal
ranges. Often, they declared war on awesome foes.

*Tue. Apr. 26. 1898. What do you think? We almost got
burned out today. Wasn't it funny? No, it was too
serious to be funny it was strange. Papa was burning brush this side of the potato patch & the fire got
out into the thick willows on the island, the wind
came up and—well we had most of our goods out on
the hill & but for the mercy of God & two men who
happened along would now be homeless. Uncle Geo.
& Dell came up after a while. Dell is almost sick. He
is going to stay all night. Our goods are all back
now & I guess we are safe.*

*Mon. Aug. 29, 1898. Mamma washed the white
clothes today. The bed-bugs have taken possession of
my room and we are fighting them with all our
might....*

Eggs were gathered, cows milked, cream churned
and butter molded; the excess was sold in town for
ready cash. Much of the produce, fresh in summer or
canned for winter, came from the garden or was part of
the wild bounty.

*Tue. July 19, 1898. I picked over 1/2 a 5 lb pail full
of goose berries some ripe and some otherwise.*

Cooking for Lora sometimes proved an adventure.

*Fri. Jan. 28, 1898. Yesterday for dinner I baked a
corn cake and it was all right only I did not put any
sugar in it.*

Inspired by an abundance of available ingredients, she
sallied into pudding making.

*Mon. Mar. 14, 1898. I am learning to cook puddings.
I can cook 4 kinds now. We have had pudding every
day for dinner lately & I made them.*

Practice must have made perfect for Lora's pudding
making, as eventually Charley Fait, a young man who
often worked for Horace and stayed with the family,
was willing to pay for her productions.

*Tue. Mar. 15, 1898. I made an Estelle pudding &
Papa & Chas. each promised me 10 cents if I would
make another for supper. I have put it over to steam
& the dip is cooking. Chas. payed [sic] me .*

Sun. Mar. 20, 1898. Uncle George came up with some Buckskin & wanted Mamma to make him some gloves. He stayed to dinner. I made an "English" Pudding.

Mon. Mar. 21, 1898. Uncle George said yesterday after dinner that my pudding was good even if I had had my feet in it. Only think!

THE MEN ARE RIDING FOR HORSES AGAIN

WHILE SHE WAS WILLING, for a price, to make Estelle pudding for Papa and Charley and saw religious commitment in helping Mamma clean house, Lora was essentially an outdoor girl. In the absence of her older brother Cliff, she was her father's compatriot on the ranch. She was acquainted with the intensive work: chopping wood, building fence, grubbing and burning brush, planting potatoes, working the broncs, haying with horses and capturing and milking the cows.

> *June 6, 1897. Mr. Fait, Lizzie & I cut potato seed all day. [The next day] Papa, Uncle Platt and I made fence.*

> *Sat. Feb. 12, 1898. ...Today Papa was grubbing brush over across the creek and just before dinner was ready I was going across to call him to dinner. When I got to the creek he was lying flat on his face on the ice above the fence. I thought he must be hurt and asked what was the matter and he said, "I am watching fish." Sure enough he had taken his ax and chopped a hole in the ice and was looking through it. He had seen some small ones but he wanted to see some large ones so I took the ax and*

*pounded the ice some but he didn't see any. He is a
great fishing crank....*

*Sun. Dec. 4, 1898. The men are riding for horses
again.*

*Wed. Dec. 14, 1898. Charley and I drove in the
bunch of horses that is in our field into the back corral, and he roped Dan. He (Dan) acted first rate and
is almost a broke horse.*

Like the horse Dan, animals of all kinds are important characters in the diary. Generally they are named,
applauded or cursed, loved and lamented. The antics of
the white rat, Tatty and the big blue Maltese, Sancho
cheered the incapacitated Lizzie. Lora recounted how
the team Jack and Joe, belonging respectively to her
father and John Cluff, had helped, by serving as both
saddle and work horses, to build the homestead; and
how her Aunt Franc was dismayed and amused by her
arrival at the Columbian Exhibition in a relative's
handsome carriage hitched to a high-stepping thor-
oughbred and a mule. On the return trip to Wyoming,
one of the teams combined the beautiful white Prince
and the ugly, dirty-gray, bumble-footed, faithful Jim.
The canary, Captain Dick (named after a Dicken's character) rode in the wagon with Lora and Lizzie.

His Royal Nibbs, the gift of Mr. Robbins and "the
most beautiful horse in the world," was the equine hero
of Lora's youth.

*June 4, 1897. Carrie and I rode on horseback. Papa
cut Nibb's bangs & mane. Lizzie rode on Prince.*

*Wed Dec. 1, 1897. I have not been out to see His
Royal Nibbs today I expect he wishes I'd come.*

Horses slowed the pace of life, as well as that of travel.

Sun. June 26, 1898. I have now to describe <u>one</u> of the pleasantest days I ever spent. I got out of bed on the wrong side this morning (though I don't see how I could for it is against the wall) and was feeling rather seedy. While we were eating breakfast, I took a notion I wanted to go up & see Aunt Nannie so after I had fed Sis, I took some oats in my dress pocket and started out to catch the pony. The horses were just above the upper cottonwoods and I fed Nibbs & Kate a little oats, then bridled Nibbs & fed Colonel a little, I led Betie up to a rye grass stump to get on and rode him up to the barn, put his saddle on him, fed him a little more oats from a sack out there led him to the house and tied him to a wagon wheel. I noticed that his mane was pretty long so I went in to ask Papa if he would cut it. He wanted to know why I didn't cut it myself. I said I was afraid I would spoil its looks but he said there was no danger so I went ahead. I didn't make a very bad job of it either. I had to take the saddle off to get at some of his mane. When I got that back on I went into the house & found Lizzie dressing up in her best "pink and white" to go to church with Charley. I helped her dress, put some roses in her hair. Then I proceeded with my own dress. I wore my blouse & black skirt. Got started at last with a yeast jug & flat iron for Aunt Nan & a roll of papers too. On top of the second "bench" or the Cushman hill I met George Garoot & Dell (who has been working in Charley's place coming down, Dell said Howdy & passed on. I saw lots of pretty flowers & things. I took a "cut-off" and had some perfectly awful roads but there all O.K. They were all glad to see me and Aunt Nan was perfectly delighted that I had brought the jug and iron. They have moved into Hassetts cabin now, *which is much nicer than the other. (Written June 27.) I got there just nicely in time for dinner and after dinner [Tad and I] rode. First we started over towards the South Fork to see the trolley. Up hill & down hill we went. There were a few cabins along the trail. By & by we came out on the valley of the river & on this side of the river is the Fait cabin & on the other side, a little farther up are 4 cabins in one of which Mr. Larsen & his wife live, I don't know any of the others. We rode up and down the river but didn't see any trolley & started back. When we had gone a little ways we saw a man on a superb bay horse dashing to the river on the other side. He crossed & came on up to see us. It was Mr. Larsen & he wanted us to go over & see his wife so we went. The river is not very high. We found her a very pleasant little person. On the way back to camp we found some columbines & picked a big bunch for Aunt Nan. I was riding astride behind the saddle & Carrie in it coming along a side hill near Camp the path went like this around a willow & we were going fast & just as Nib turned the corner he got out of the path a little & stepped in a big dog-hole & fell flat on his side luckily hurting "nothin' nor nobody" But don't tell or it will worry Mamma and Aunt Nannie. When we got back to camp and delivered the columbines to Aunt Nannie, we turned around & rode over to the mine. Mike Hassett's mine is about half a mile down the hill to one side of the Blue Bell and we walked down. Jack Donlan, one of the men that was at Gold Hill last winter, is working there & so is Elmer Andrews. It was an awful climb back up the hill but we made it. We stayed there at the mine a few minutes & then went to camp and I went home.*

Lora at one time feared she had lost Nibbie to the harness.

> *Tue. Mar. 14, 1899. Papa is going to drive Nibbie this morning. O dear!! 5.45 P.M. Nibbie did well and so good-bye saddle pony.*

In reality, although she frequently loaned His Royal Nibbs, he remained uniquely Lora's.

The dog Trix was the shared pet of Lora and Charley Fait.

> *June 8, 1897. This morning Lizzie, Carrie, Trix and I went picnicking and got home about noon.*

> *Oct. 29. Trix is happy with Charlie up at the sawmill.*

> *Tues. Dec. 21, 1897. I hope Charley will bring Trix when he comes. He said he would.*

> *Sun. Jan. 2, 1898. We went sleigh-riding with Charlie and instead of driving Major with Peggy, we drove Frank with her and they go better together for a fast team. Papa, Mamma, Charley, Lizzie and I all went and Trix went too & capered along in high glee.*

But Trix did not continue "in high glee."

> *Sat. Jan. 22, 1898. Papa and Charley lost Trix yesterday & Papa says he hoped she stayed lost.*

> *Wed. Feb. 9, 1898. Trix is sick she has been sick for 3 or 4 days.*

Sat. March 5, 1898. Trix is dead. She won't go with me to carve L.N. on the trees again. I framed with strips of pasteboard the head of an angel last night.

+Wed. Apr. 6, 1898. I dug Trix out of the snow drift where she has been & buried her in the old snake-head-blue-bell patch. I named the place "Little Trixie Park"

Thu. Apr. 28, 1898. Southy has got a dog a nice sensible one that Papa wants and he said (Papa was telling us this evening) "Well, I'll tell you, I'll give her to the littlest girl." That's me, won't it be fine? Her name is "Sis"...Just wait 'til I get Sis. Won't I be proud. I intend to plant some "mariposa" lilies on Trixie's grave next summer. Little Trixie Park will be very nice if kept in order.

With good humor, young Lora was ready to attempt any job on the ranch, yet evidently she was never required or coerced into doing anything. Her parents were the most gentle of mentors. They acknowledged that both she and Lizzie were entitled to childhoods; no circumstance was allowed to interfere with this. During the first stay in Wyoming, when the girls were little more than toddlers, their entertainment was primary to Horace as he devised games and diversions, out of nothing, for their benefit. Assured that medicine could do no more for Lizzie's displaced hip, the Nichols returned to Wyoming partly because Lizzie, in Lora's words, "was so homesick for the dear old ranch." Both Horace and Sylvia tried to assure that Lizzie's life would be as normal as possible. Neither the diary nor *I Remember* records disharmony in the Nichols family. Although Lora often reacted emotionally as she penned freshly occurring events, anger at Lizzie or at their parents was, with one exception, totally absent from Lora's daily account.

TODAY IS THE DAY
THEY GIVE BABIES AWAY
WITH HALF A POUND OF TEA

THE NICHOLS PLAYED the usual popular parlor games of the day. Card games, like Pedro, sluff and solo, were favorites with the family and other folks along the creek. Lora maintained cribbage was her papa's tool for instructing her in arithmetic.

> *Thu. Feb. 17, 1898. Charley & I played a game of chess. I am teaching him.*

But for sheer celebration of family solidarity, creativity, and joy, nothing compared with Christmas.

> *Sat. Dec. 18, 1897. Hello. Papa wired two of our chairs together today in a very solid & satisfactory manner. I read a book by the name of "Within an ace." My dolls Christmas progresses finely. I must go after the tree soon. Papa & Mamma shut themselves into the kitchen today and Christmassed (a word of my invention). A day or two ago Papa fixed an Indian Sled & we Papa & I hauled wood on it. Yesterday Lizzie got her new fiddle-box & other things & something she put in her doll trunk I am not to see. I wonder what it is. Papa put the new head in Lizzie's banjo yesterday. It sounds much bet-*

*ter. I believe now that December is the best month of
the year. Dear Nibbs is as gentle as anything now
and always whinnies when he sees me.*

Beginning in 1896—the last Boulder Christmas
spent in Grandma Nichols' "pompous red plush parlor"—Lora recorded a lifetime of such occasions. The
doll Grandfather Nichols wanted the dismayed Lora to
name "Dorcas," now renamed "Isabel," played an important part in the following year's holiday on the ranch.

*Dec. 25, 1897. We went to bed at 10.15 last night and
got up about an hour before daylight. I got a commode with a verse:*

You've got a thimble for your hand
And a cloth to wipe your nose
But this will answer for a stand
And a place to put your clothes.

and I got a chair for Isabel; it said—

If any ask you whose I am
'Tis better not to tell
But if you *have* to why just say
For Baby Isabel.

Lizzie and I got a bookcase together & the verse is

To make a bookcase for each girl
Was more than I could do
And so I made one big enough
To hold the books of *two.*

*Lizzie made me a pair of bloomers. I have them on
now & a shirtwaist & an old tie of Papa's. The
label—*

Them's her lovely bloomers, Mister,
Yep & they're real.

*I got a white cotton underwaist like I wanted and
the label—*

Lora. I didn't make any more like this.
For fear it would be too small.
But if this one fits, I'll make some more
& put trimming on them all. Mother.

Lizzie made me a doll dress for Violet and wrote

Miss Violet McCarthy dressed up for the party
In farthingale bodice & frill.

*And then Mamma made me the sweetest little white
"poke" bonnet for Belle and the label said—*

On Little Baby Isabel
I'd write a pretty sonnet
If my mind was not so taken up
Admiring her new bonnet.

I also had a little shelf with a bracket that looked like
a Negro's face, a tablet & a calendar & nuts & candy
galore. And I got a pretty pin cushion. Lizzie got a
commode (new kind) a shelf a pen-wiper a letter case,
a pair of half sleeves. Mamma got a lot of squares,
two iron-holders, two aprons & two handkerchiefs.
Papa got a muffler, a flute box, a subscription to the
weekly News, a bottle of perfume (New Mown Hay),
& a pair of gloves. I had my doll Christmas tree this
morning...It was lovely. Violet looked lovely in her
new dress.

Beyond the private world of the Nichols' homestead
was the next social structure, the neighborhood defined

by the creek, the North Fork of the Encampment River. John Cluff, who had come down from his mountain claim to join Horace on the flat creek bottom and shared in every way the difficulties of those first years, had moved on to become a businessman in Saratoga. The Fleming family occupied his ranch. Gene and Dell, the Fleming boys, appeared often at the Nichols' place, christened "Willow Glen" by Lora. Their sister Lindy, who married George Herring and became the mother of a growing flock of lively boys, "cared for" Lora when Lora's parents went to Saratoga to the dentist.

It was a shared love of music that bound Dell to Lora and her family.

> +*Nov. 11. In the evening the Willow Glen Band was out in full force. Dell, Papa, Lizzie and I.*

> +*Sunday Dec. 12, 1897. Dell is here and he & Lizzie are playing their* <u>violins</u>*...dear I wish I could play my banjo with Dell & Lizzie.*

Lora acknowledged that Lizzie had "the gift of music"; Lizzie and Dell sometimes played "seconds" at dances. Lora kept working on her repertoire and admitted,

> *Mon. Jan. 17, 1898. I wish someone would offer me a job picking second just to see how quick I'd snap them up.*

> *Tue. June 21, 1898. ...Mr. Herring & Dell were up this forenoon and Dell fiddled for us. One of his suspenders kept coming off and Lizzie said, "Dell if I were you I'd take a couple of pegs and drive in my shoulders. That would hold them on." But he said he usually had two girls, one hanging on each shoulder.*

*Lib started to say "widows, you mean," but he was
too quick for her.*

Lora could have picked second, perhaps even first,
if the old-time country dances of her childhood were
still occurring. But those all-night dances, where families arrived from miles around at some ranch house
and "where every talent was called upon" for entertainment, had been replaced. With the establishment
of Grand Encampment City, a new sophistication came
into the valley. The Nichols could not have anticipated
on May 20, 1897, as they passed the embryo town on
their return to the ranch, the changes that town would
bring to their lives and those of their ranching neighbors. Often, the social dance introduced the rural community to the motley folk flocking to the mining district.

In the early pages of *I Remember* Lora recalled one
of her first dances at Grand Encampment, her introduction to Carl Ashley, the new postmaster's son, and
his creative costuming at later masquerades.

The big St. Patrick's Ball was held that year of
1898 in the newly finished building on Freeman
Avenue which was known for years as Allen's Hall
and which answered the purpose of a ball-room
before the City Hall was built. For several reasons I
remember that dance very well; it was well attended,
the music was good and everyone seemed in a merry
mood. A lot of green bunting was in evidence too, in
honor of the saint of the Emerald Isle, and Dad who
was floor manager that night, came down the floor
where many sets of a quadrille were kicking up their
heels, to the one where I was dancing, and said to me,
"See that boy in the green bunting breeches up on
the platform there?" And when I signified that I *did,*

Mrs. Ashley, as Pocahantas

he added, "That's Ashley's kid." Dad and Mr. Hank Ashley who had established the first rooming house in the town had become fast friends, and he had told me that Mr. Ashley had sent for his family, consisting of his wife daughter and son. It seems they arrived just in the nick of time to attend the big Ball....

Those Minstrel Men
Joe McNamara, Byron Tillou, and Frank Lordier at a
Thanksgiving masquerade in 1899.

Although that St. Pat's costume was the first he
sported at dances in town, it was far from the last!
On one occasion, [Carl] appeared as a Zulu chief,
practically sans garments, with the exception of a
skirt of palm fronds; Mrs. Ashley complained, "Hank
Ashley cut *all* the leaves off my palm to make that
suit."

I think the best costume Carl ever wore though
was at a masquerade where he dressed as Mabel
Wilcox, the "cutest" girl in the valley; he dressed just
as she usually appeared at the dances, in a pretty little white dress with her dark hair crimped and
falling loose over her shoulders. He copied her every
little mannerism to perfection; she had a way of
swinging her skirts as she walked, tossing back her
hair and pushing her puff sleeves up occasionally.
When it came near supper-time when the dancers

Horace Nichols and Miranda Shafe
This pair provided entertainment at the old-time ranch parties.
Miranda played an organ which was hauled in a wagon from one
party to another.

would unmask, Mr. Ashley came over to the set
where I was, and asked, "Have you spotted Carl yet?"

I shook my head and he said, "He is dancing in
this set right beside you." Well, I cast a look at the
set, and every one of the four men dancing there was
old, or fat, or tall, and couldn't possibly be Carl. I
looked back at Mr. Ashley for an explanation and he
pointed at *Mabel Wilcox* dancing right by me. Most of
us had not even given a second glance, merely wondered to ourselves "I wonder why Mabel didn't mask.
Just wearing a domino." When the signal came to
unmask, I never saw so many surprised looks.

(IR, 56)

Glass plate, photographer unknown
Theatrical production at Grand Encampment City

*Sat. June 11, 1898. How fine! Papa told us last
night of a "calico ball" to be held at Encampment,
Monday night. Every girl is to wear calico at least a
calico waist and make a tie to match. The men all
grab a tie and then hunt up the girl whose waist
matches the tie and then she is his partner. Won't
that be fun? I am wondering who will be my partner.
I hope it will be someone nice.....Lizzie has her calico
tie made. She is going to wear her yellow waist and
I am going to wear my "Aunt Mary shally" [sic] &
make the tie out of part of the skirt. Mamma is
going to wear Lizzie's red waist.*

*Mon. June 13, 1898. "Today is the day they give
babies away with a half a pound of tea. There'll be a
hot time in the old town tonight." The dance is to be*

*in Allen's Hall...I wonder who my partner for
tonight will be. I hope not Mulstey.*

*Tue. June 14, 1898. Well, the dance was fine. Who do
you suppose got my tie. The Encampment butcher
whom it would be easier to jump over than to walk
around him. But he is a good partner.*

HE HAS KISSED AND KISSED HER
ONCE, TWICE, THRICE—
AND THEN SOME

THE NEWLY EMERGED CENTER of the Grand Encampment Mining District had a surfeit of single men or men with absent families; this didn't deter an active social agenda. At the festivities in the new town, Lora, at fourteen, was expected to take her place with the older girls and women, being a partner in dancing and in taking the traditional midnight supper.

At the same time, when she and Lizzie resumed their school careers, they were obliged to ride beyond Grand Encampment City, which as yet had no school building, to attend the rural school in the village of Doggett. School there in the fall of 1897 was a three-month school; at the turn of the century in rural Wyoming, school could occur any time of the year and for any length of time, usually depending upon the availability of a teacher and a meeting place. Cold weather and snow during this session especially hampered Lora and Lizzie's attendance.

> *Oct. 24, 1897. ...Lizzie saw our school teacher yester-*
> *day...Our teacher Mr. Fagan is nice.*

++ *Oct. 26. Yesterday we went to school. Warm in morning. Froze coming home, snowed from 4 o'clock. So snowy and cold couldn't go today....*

Oct. 29. I went to school today and I had a nice time. Guy helped me with my horse. I washed poor Frankie's face. Dave got into a quarrel with Jesse Brownly. Teacher said my composition was fine. Guy lent me a lead pencil. We read Words, by John Ruskin for supplementary reading and had a physiology lesson. I brought home the paper doll Mabel gave me. Jimmy my boy rode up with me as far as Doggett. Had a chat with Frank and Amos Belle L. Love them that hate you. Nibbs let me catch him easy...I like Mr. Fagan very well and Cousin Guy is fine. Dearest my gnilrad Knarf is so nice.

Nov. 1. I went to school today. Belle and Edna are mad again. Jimmie rode up again. I guess Frank and Amos are not mad. I hope not. Clara & Lot devoted champions.

Nov. 2. Went to school. Belle Edna and company's rebel gang still holds out. Parr & I are on the go. I'm to take gnilrad a paper doll.

Nov. 3. Took paper doll to gnilrad. Am to take more. Made up with B & E. Got my riding whip again.

+*Nov. 5. Yesterday I didn't go to school. Today I did. I'm to go to Wilcox's tomorrow. Cold. Tr. says I'm to enlarge "Our Schoolhouse" for exercises. I rode Nibbs to school. I got up cows. Dell is here this evening. Dodger's neck tie is tied. Didn't take a doll for gnilrad. Wolfards swiped his. I am going to ask Mamma if I can send for more. D. Dye.*

Lizzie on the horse lot fence

*+Nov. 18. I went to school all of this week, so far.
Teacher's music books came and we are learning a
song. Learn a little every day. The Wilcox children
were at school yesterday and today. I brought
Tommy and Johnny Peryam with me to their house
and then brought Jimmie on up to Dogget and then
Gene rode from Dogget up to the ranch with me.
Hurrah! A dance at Dogget on Tuesday evening...I
am to invite the whole school. Ira Dodger, Ginty and
Amos had a fight over who should hitch up my
horse. O dear! I wish they liked each other. Teacher
asked Belle Edna and me to sing a song for three
girls. He will show us the song.*

*Wed. Dec. 22, 1897. Well. Hello again, how are you.
Lizzie and I have been down to school to get my
books. We think now, but do not know, that we will
go to the school entertainment. Mr. Fagan wants me*

to write a composition about our school-house and Lizzie is to play her banjo....

After the entertainment, the scholars were turned out until the next fall. For Lizzie, this session with Mr. Fagan as teacher marked the end of her school career.

Sun. March 21, 1898. It snowed a little bit this morning and is cold. I wrote to Josie yesterday. Mamma wants to wash Wed. if possible to wash Charley's white shirt & my white waist. Lizzie showed me a note yesterday from Charley. It said "Allow one to thank you dear for the flowers." He gave it to her while I was making pudding & Papa & Mamma were both there. He has kissed & kissed her once, twice—thrice & then some....

Although Charley had been part of the Nichols' homestead almost since the moment of their return, Lora seemed unaware of the mutual attraction between Lizzie and Charley. Lora's first reaction to their romance was one of playful anger.

Mon. June 6, 1898. I don't want Charley to marry Libsey he isn't good enough. Now if I was only old enough and nice enough so "Georgie" would think "summat" of me why "there'd be a hot time in old town." [A day later] Lib says she is going to marry Charley. Horrors! I wish he had never come near us.

With the passage of a few days and an intervention by Mamma, Lora recorded a change of heart.

Fri. June 10, 1898. I don't know whether I object to Charley for a brother any more than I would anyone else. Mamma says when Libsey is gone I can have her room for a sitting room. Won't that be nice?

Spring Ranch
Charley and Lizzie's home

Lizzie's engagement was six months long and, as the wedding day slowly approached, Lora was drawn into the excitement of the plans.

Fri. June 17, 1898. The Spring Ranch is as good as gotten for Charley and there are others.

Wed. June 22, 1898. Charley came from the hills early this morning before anyone but Lizzie was up. She said she would not have been if she had thought he was coming. Papa and Mamma went up yesterday to tell him he must go to Saratoga today to make a dicker with Abe Fingerly for the Spring ranch over towards Cow Creek. Abe picks a couple of

Papa's bunch
Abe Fingerly picked two, as a trade for the Spring Ranch

*horses out of Papa's bunch, then Charley pays Papa
for the horses and gets the ranch that is the bargain.
Charley took with him to Saratoga to mail, an order
to Montgomery Ward and Co. Chicago for gloves for
Mamma, Lib and I and fishing tackle for the men
and an order to J. Lynn & Co. 48 Bond Street N.Y.
for—what do you suppose—an engagement ring! It
is a $2.00 one and the premiums are a breast-pin for
Mamma and an opal ring for me. An opal is the
October birthstone is why I want that ring....*

That fall the school was in session again in the
building at Doggett. As Lora's mother was a director, it
was her responsibility to secure a teacher for the district.

Tue. Oct. 4, 1898. About six inches of snow on the ground and still falling. Sunday night Mamma sent Dave with a note to Cora Fairchilds to start school the next day if she could. Charley was down this morning on Betie (he got him to water Dan with). and he says she has started. I am going over to see if Nora knows it has started. I will go pretty soon...Charley has got some shoes and put on Nibs. Wasn't he good? Mamma & Papa are putting down the carpet.

Lora, without the companionship of Lizzie, now rode to school with the Herring children who were staying across the lane with the Flemings.

Wed. Oct. 5, 1898. I am going to school this morning. I am all ready. It is 7.45. Charley has just gone to water Dan with Nibs then I will start at 8.15 about. It is night now. I got along at school alright. Miss Fairchild is fine. There was quite a school...

Mon. Oct. 17, 1898. I went to school, bought some bird-seed and two yards of dress-lining. Mamma is making me a blue pressed flannel Eton Suit with a red vest and didn't have lining enough. Papa drove little Colonel to Doggett and got a stall of Jack Allsup (he runs the livery barn) to put my pony in....

Wed. Oct. 19, 1898. ...Our school-house leaks and is "pesky uncomfortable." Lib says to write that her and Charley are foolish but they are not. They are all right.

Sat. Oct. 22, 1898. I have cleaned my ponies' stable, wiped the dishes and given the bird his bath. Did you know I was two people? I am Miss Nichols and "The Kid." I am the Kid at home and Miss Nichols elsewhere....

Sun. Oct. 23, 1898. ...Well, what do you suppose?
Our teacher, Cora Fairchild, has become Mrs. Lyman
Sparks!! Charley went to town this afternoon and
came back with that news....

Mon. Oct. 24, 1898. Cora was married on Saturday.
I went to school of course and who do you suppose I
sit with now? Cousin Dave. They are crowded and
the teacher (<u>Mrs. Sparks</u>) wanted me to so of course I
made no objections. We had three new scholars this
morning Albert and Burley Hoge (he spells it Burley)
and Harry Dunlap. I will try and tell you all of the
scholars. Violet and Florence Cummings, Alice, Lura,
Annie and Bartlett Alsup, Jimmie and Clara
Fairchilds, Jennie and Carl Ashley, Mamie Harry,
Cyrus and Paul Dunlap, Alice and Raymond
Waumbaker, Burton and Perry Culleton, Dave, Guy
and Keene Nichols, Nora Ola, Leila and Esther
Herring, and Ellice Herring and me. Little Maggie
Culleton is going to come soon. Haven't we quite a
school....

Tue. Nov. 15, 1898. I went to school yesterday and
today. Nora rides Billy to school now. She started to
go on Monday, and I go on Nibs. I go by Lindy's and
Nora and I cross on the bridge. We take turns carry-
ing Ellis on behind us and the one that don't have
Ellis on behind, must let down the bars.

Tue. Nov. 22, 1898. I went to school and it was terri-
bly cold. When I got there I felt one of my sick
headaches coming on so I came back. I pretty near
froze and when I got here I wasn't sick at all....

The remainder of the winter term faded for Lora.
She briefly mentions that teacher hoped she could

come to do a piece for the program but Lora never mentioned doing this or returning to school. She wrote forcefully of that year's winter.

> *Fri. Feb. 3, 1899. The weather is awful blowing like a grampus and, to use an expressive though very, very inelegant expression, is as cold as Death's pecker hung in a well.*

> *Wed. Feb. 8, 1899. Day before yesterday morning Billy Mulsty's thermometer got down to 44 below zero and then froze up.*

While Lora was fighting the winter in her attempt to attend school at Doggett, Lizzie and Charley's arrangements were moving apace.

> *Fri. Nov. 25, 1898. ...We started, Charley and Lizzie in the buggy behind Dan and Peggy and I on Nibbs, at about ten o'clock to go over and see Charley's ranch. It is a dear little place and (which I expect would shock Mrs. Grundy if she should hear of it) we went inside and it is lovely....*

> *Mon. Dec. 5, 1898. The license arrived. It is snowing blue blazes. Charley, Papa and Dell are handling broncs. Charley is going over to his ranch tonight. It is snowing but he must go because his Sunday clothes are over there and he can't very well be married in his shirt-tail.*

> *Tue. Dec. 6, 1898. Today, O today is the Fait L. wedding day. Will Peryam performed the ceremony and then we ate a cracker-jack of a dinner. They are gone now over to the ranch and we are "batching" or so it seems.*

Studio Portrait

The Fait–L Wedding Day

So Lizzie, almost seventeen and still using her crutch, became the bride of Charley Fait. They moved to the Spring Ranch, two miles north of Grand Encampment and riding cross-country, just a bit farther than that from the homestead at Willow Glen.

Lizzie assumed all the chores of the ranch wife, both in the two-story log house and at the barn.

Thu. Dec. 8, 1898. ...I was over to see Lib this after-noon and she is well settled and getting along famously. It seems so queer to have her in separate establishments.

I HAVE BEEN "IN LOVE"
ABOUT 100 TIMES SINCE I WAS A BABY

DURING THE COURSE of Lizzie and Charley's romance, Diary was the recipient of Lora's musings on courtship, marriage, and childbearing.

> +Sat. May 28, 1898. ...I always say & sometimes think that I want to be an old maid because I don't think it would be right for me to bring children into this world to suffer from any weakness I have but, deep down in my heart there is a wish for a home of my own and I know no <u>man</u> would agree to such a condition.

> Sun. Sept. 4, 1898. Lizzie and I went to see Shorty and Gold today and stayed all day. They seem so happy and nice. I believe greatest happiness must be in a husband, for women. Now don't laugh I would really like to marry some dear good man and "live happily ever afterward."

Lora was poised at the precarious line between childhood and adulthood. At home she was regularly playing with dolls.

> Mon. June 13, 1898. I have lots of fun playing with my dolls. I have Violet, Mae, Dan, and Johnny,

*Harry, Molly, Pearl, Ed and Nannie, nine of them
and I play with Lizzie's, Rosa, Ida, Jack, Sallie and
Carol and Fanny (six).*

*Thu. June 16, 1898. I made a lot on my dolls' plea-
sure road today. I made ten lengths of fence which is
quite a good deal as you may imagine, I made it
with the hoe. I looked in my arithmetic to find out
how much a doll mile was and it is quite a lot more
than I thought it was. I am in II Samuel in my Bible
now. I have a great time playing. I expect if folks
knew I played with dolls they would be surprised.*

She reported with horror that her clothes were to
announce her growing up.

*Sun. Oct. 23, 1898. Mamma is making my dresses
down to my shoe tops now. O dear! She says next
summer they shall be longer still.*

Simultaneously, Lora conspired with Cousin Carrie
and Lizzie so that she made the proper appearance at
a ball. Her menses (which she called variously
"unwell," "coming around," or, usually and simply, "Z")
could produce a reaction of dramatic prostration or
total indifference.

About the time Lizzie declared her intention to
marry Charley, Lora confided to diary, "I have been 'in
love' about 100 times since I was a baby" (Wed. May 25,
1898). Now with Lizzie's example before her, she was
certainly in love with the older George Brown, generally noted as *he* in the diary.

*+Fri. June 3, 1898. Hip Hurrah! George Brown isn't
going to war after all! Mamma said he couldn't be
colonel or whatever it was he wanted to be so he did-
n't go. I am glad. Some ill disposed person has start-*

ed a scandal about him and Goldy. They say the rea-
son he went to war so suddenly is because Goldy is
getting larger then is natural. But I hadn't noticed
anything wrong with her and even if there was I
wouldn't believe it of him....

Sat. Jan. 21, 1899. I am at home now. I came over
yesterday afternoon. It is 10 A.M. We went to the
dance and all had a fine time. He was there and I
danced with him several times and had one long,
delicious waltz with him....

Sun. Jan. 22, 1899. It was cloudy this forenoon and
started to snow pretty hard about noon, shortly
afterward I started down to see Clella and I took my
skates. She asked at the dance to come. It wasn't so
very cold though it was snowy. When I got there, who
do you suppose was there. Why Him! So we went
skating above the Dunkard Dam. Goldy and Shorty,
Dick Nolan, Albert Hoge, Him, Clella and I were all
of the crowd. Dick built a fire close to the bank (He
asked him to though) in a nice little sheltered nook.
We had a lovely time (because he was there) and as I
was coming home, I came by Dell's and he came up
to our house. Papa and Mamma went to Doggett and
got home just after Dell & I.

Wed. Feb. 1, 1899. Went to Lib's today intending to
stay but Lib and I came in the sled to Doggett with
Charley and came up home and are here now to stay
all night. It has been snowing steadily all day. Oh!
dear!! He is deeply in love with Clella and I'm a fool
and its a nice muddle all round and I love him!

The "nice muddle" later cleared when Lora and Clella
Fairchild became best friends and Lora wrote, "I could
dance at *his* wedding with a heart as light as my heels
for he is a darling" (Tue. Feb. 7, 1899).

The following month, Lora fell in love for time 102.

*+Sat. Mar. 18, 1899. 9 A.M. We went to the hop last
night and had a fine time. Libsey and Charley came
over yesterday afternoon and they rode down with
us. Annie is at Dell's and Elmer, Annie, Papa ,
Mamma Dell and I rode in the little wagon with
Dell's team. A fellow lent us some magazines. His
name is Oldman or something like that. Clella and
Mr. Brown were not there. Billy Wilcox and Ned
Green played and Dell had a lay off which he made
the most of. Dell wants us to go singing tomorrow
night. I don't know whether we will or not. And
Oldman is coming up someday (This is on the Q.T.)
I don't know how Mamma will like it but I couldn't
help it as he as good as invited himself. 4.30 P.M. I
went down and got the mail (I didn't get any and
saw Bert, I mean Mr. Oldman).*

Bert Oldman was, in Lora's words, "a fellow"
because he was a stranger to the valley, part of the
incoming flow of speculators, prospectors, and miners
arriving in the Grand Encampment Mining District.
An Englishman, he had arrived from the Colorado
Springs area; he hoped to get a head start on the developments. Many of the mining properties, those around
the new town of Battle on the Continental Divide and
also the first-developed Ferris Haggarity Mine, were
reached by traveling up the Finley Hill, which was literally in the Nichols' backyard. Therefore, Bert's business ramblings plus the social activities at Grand
Encampment City gave him a unique opportunity to
court young Lora. But it was natural that Bert was
regarded as an interloper by Papa and the other folks
on the creek, especially neighbor Dell Fleming, who
was spending as much time as possible at Willow Glen.

Thu. Mar. 30, 1899. Dell is up playing solo.

Tue. Apr. 4, 1899. We went to the dance but George and Lindy did not go Something got wrong with the baby at the last minute so they couldn't go just Papa, Mamma, Dell and I went in the little wagon.

Wed. Apr. 5, 1899. Dell was up this afternoon to get the brace and bit and asked me to be his partner at the next dance.

Lora vowed on April 8, "The folks down here just treat BO mean. I just bet I'll be as good as pie to him."

Mon. Apr. 24, 1899. ...This morning as Mum and I were sitting in the front room discussing the new house. BO rode up to the door and stopped a minute or two, on his way to the hills. This evening as he came down he stopped and talked to Pop (who was cutting wood) for a little while.

+Wed. May 3, 1899. ...Today Bo came by on his way up to the hills and left us some magazines. I saw him but he didn't see me. I ran when I saw him coming because I had omitted to curl my bangs.

Mon. May 8, 1899. 10.30 A.M. Bo and another man have just gone by into the hills. 6.30 P.M. ...Dear Bert (for shame) has just been here a few minutes on the way to the hills and left me some magazines and candy.

+Sat. June 17. 4.30 A.M. Just got home from the dance a few minutes ago. I am going to bed. 1 P.M. Now I will tell about the dance. Yesterday, after school, Carrie and I went up on the hill and got a lot of "dog tooth violets" and made them into bouquets. I had promised to bring Jen and her beau, Mayme

and hers and Mrs. Ashley, all a bouquet. Papa,
Mamma, Carrie Dell and I all went down in the lit-
tle wagon. I put bouquets on Dell, Papa and Mum.
Carrie and I too of course. When we got there I gave
Nora, Mrs. Doc Culleton, Libsey and Bo one. Bo was
my partner, poor Dell was just too late and he ate
supper with Nora which tickled her most to death.
The Wilcox girls were over. Libsey gave me her fan.
Wasn't she good? And (something about Bert) I had
a rose-geranium leaf which I had worn all night
and he asked for it so I gave it to him and he put it
in his "weskit pocket." "Rediculous! " 8 P.M. Carrie
and I rode horseback.

During the summer of 1899, Lora, "the kid," continued at school while "Miss Nichols" became more infat-
uated with Bert Oldman. The two month's session with
Nell Bennett as teacher and companion was the apex of
Lora's school career at Doggett.

Tue. June 6, 1899. I went to school. It started yester-
day but I didn't know it. Miss Nellie Bennett is
teacher.

Fri. June 9, 1899. We got out of school at half past
three. Carrie rode Nib and I rode Eagle. When we
went to saddle our horses, Eagle was gone and we
thought he had got loose (they were picketed) and
Guy was going to put my saddle in Pretty's barn and
I was going to walk but Frank Cunningham wasn't
going to let me walk and just as he was going to
saddle a horse Pierce came out and said that Papa
had traded Eagle off for a bay horse and left it there.
So he went and got it & I rode it home. A big bay
and quite easy.

Wed. June 14, 1899. 8 P.M. Carrie and I went to
school on Frank (the new horse) and Nibs, Frank got

*away and rolled in the ditch and plastered himself
with mud from end to end but we caught him again.
Will Foreman, Pretty and Frank Cunningham are
getting up a dance for Friday night. "Yum! Yum!"*

*Wed. July 5, 1899. 4.30 A.M. Just got home. Our pic-
nic yesterday was a success....Bo and Red got up a
dance for the evening and it was fine. A big crowd &
good music....Bo was my "Juth of 4ly" partner you
know. ("Yez" knew) I had a gay time. 8.30 P.M. This
afternoon, Bert came by on his way up to Miner
Creek, and I was down in the grove & he stopped
and talked quite a while.*

*Thu. July 6. I went over to Libsey's today and stayed
until after supper. She washed today. Mamma is Z.
Bo told me one day he has a claim on Miner Creek
named after me.*

*Fri. July 7, 1899. 11.20 A.M. Mum and I worked in
the garden this morning. Bo came up to see if I
wouldn't keep Duke [Bert's big, black dog] while he
went to Battle. I wanted to awful bad but Mum did-
n't think I'd better on Pop's account. He don't like Bo
anyway and then when he gets mad at a dog he is
liable to knock him around with a chut and I would-
n't have anything like that happen to Duke for anything. Bo stood in the yard and talked to me a while
after he started away. He left me a sack of candy
and picked me a rose. 8.30 P.M. O Gosh! (Them's my
"sentyments".) Mamma and Papa have just got back
from the P.O. and this is the result.*

Encampment, Wyo.
July 6th, 1899,
Mr. Ira O. Wolfard requests the pleasure of Miss Lora
Nichols' company at dinner next Sunday at his home.
July 9th.

Well that's not so worse. Yesterday when I went over to Lib's I saw Ira and he said he had sent it. and for me not to be surprised if it wasn't worded correctly for the boys were bothering when he wrote it. He needn't have been so ceremonious though. But listen to this—!

Encampment, Wyo.
July 7th 99.
Dear Miss Lora,
I write to ask you for your company next Sunday to go to Mr. Wolfard's for singing. I will be there at 2 o'clock. Now please let me know. Leave word in the P.O. by noon Sun.
Your well wishing Admirer
S.A. Yost.

Wouldn't that kill you?

+Tue. July 11, 1899. Went to school yesterday. Am Z today but went to school. Miss Bennett is coming up to board with us. Isn't that nice?

Wed. July 12, 1899. 8 P.M. This morning it was raining and as I am Z, I could hardly ride Nibs down in the rain so Papa hitched up little Colonel and the cart and took me. Miss Bennett waylaid him and asked him if he knew of anyone who would bring her trunk up to our house as she wanted to come up today. He didn't so he said as he had to come down after me, he would come with the team and bring it himself. Everything went off as usual only a fight between Dave and Albert Hoge. And after school, Pop came for us (Nell and the trunk and me). We got home alright and Carrie and Bessie Wheeler are here too. Bessie's father was going to the mines so they came. They will stay a week I guess. This evening after supper, Nell and I drove little Colonel down after the mail and had a gay time.

Thu. July 20, 1899. The other day Pop traded Gray Colonel to Uncle Platt for his little saddle horse he got from the gypsies. I rode him to school today and he is a cracker-jack. Beg pardon, I should say a biscuit john.

Tue. August 1, 1899. Went to school. Got a letter from Clella. Nell has some bicycle boots that came tonight. She looks cute as wax in them. Lib is still here. Charley was over Saturday & stayed till Sunday. Nell has a school at Elk Mountain beginning Sept. 11 so she hasn't a very long vacation.

Mon. Aug. 7, 1899. Nell and I walked to school and coming home we rode from Encampment up and, Oh! in such a way! Ot Husten & Pretty were on horses and they said, "Always room for one more" and slid off back of the saddles and we "clim" on and rode that way all of the way home & had a gay time. 8.20 P.M. Just as supper was ready Aunt Nan & Tad came so we'll have lots of fun. Tad & I went to Cloud City after supper.

Wed. Aug. 9. School is out. I am about half glad and half sorry. Nell went to Toga this evening. Saw Bert this evening and said "Hello" to him....

Sun. Aug. 27, 1899. 9.20 A.M. Well! I'm mad! This morning when Carrie & I went to water the horses, Nib was untied, his halter rope wound around his neck. One bridle had been used and he was still sweaty from being ridden; my saddle latigoes were undone and Nib seemed tired. Just think! I have to take him to Encampment today too.

7.50 P.M. I'm home, of course, and—well I can't begin at the beginning because I've got something so nice to tell. As I was riding along by those trees on the road past Encampment, I was thinking about Bert and I thought as it was Sunday he would be down from Battle and maybe I would get to see him. I happened (?) to glance up toward the hill between the ranch and Encampment and I saw someone and a black dog and I thought maybe he was waiting for me because he was walking around on top of the hill, and even if he wasn't I wanted to see him because—well, because I love him. When I got up there it was him and I stopped and he said he had something to tell me and—well he said a lot and said he loved me and asked me if I loved him and I said—I don't know what I said.

Mon. Aug. 28, 1899. ...Bert said his mines were turning out good. I am so glad. He deserves success after all his trouble. I am glad he told me he loves me, because now I'm happy. It's so nice to have someone to love. He said he would move down from Battle to Encampment sometime soon and then I will see him oftener. 8 P.M. I went down and sat on my old roost between the pasture fence and the creek this afternoon and got to thinking about Bert (as if I hadn't been thinking of him all day) and couldn't quit...Just think! Last winter Bert thought I might be going to marry Dell! Dell! Why just think of it! Well what does it matter? I'm not. I got a letter from Cliff tonight.

9.10 I am all ready for bed. Bert said he would try and be down this week.

Tue. Aug. 29, 1899. ...8 P.M. I'm lonesome and have the blues in the worst way. Sunday, Bert told me his birthday was yesterday, the 28th. He is 30. O dear! Now I love him lots but I wish. O I don't see.

One objection to the romance—that of Bert's being an outsider—had been almost overcome in the eyes of everyone except Papa; Grand Encampment had become a village of outsiders and the social melting pot had been perking differences away. But Bert's age, thirty, added a formidable new obstacle to the romance.

There appeared in the diary at this time a love never mentioned before, never recorded in *I Remember*. His name was Jack. He died, and his memory recurred to Lora in moments of melancholy for several years. Jack may have been a remnant of a childhood fixation or a product of reality expanded by the reading of too many sentimental novels. In the diary Jack was associated with the "demon memory" and the horse "Goldfinder." In addition, Lora felt great pressure to keep the secret of Jack to herself, especially from Bert.

Sun. Sept. 3, 1899. It is Sunday. I wonder whether Bert will come or not. It is a good day for haying only windy.

The following note was pinned into the diary.

Sunday P.M. You told me once I could always read your diary and this afternoon I did, and saw all about Bert. Oh Kid, Kid; why didn't you tell me? I told you. Was you afraid, or was you too happy to tell, just yet? Of course I won't tell, since I found out accidentally. But I'd pluck grit off a bush somewhere, and tell it to Mamma, if I was you, kidlet. Lizzie

8.20 P.M. You see what Lib has written, she knows. O I've thought & thought and I'm worn out. That demon Memory has conquered. I wish I'd never been born or else God would let me die, now. O what's the matter with me.

Mon. Sept. 4, 1899. ...O my demon! Will I ever con-
quer him. Why can't I? It won't matter to Bert even if
I tell him and he will never know if—O God.

Mon. Jan. 29, 1900. We washed. It is snowing a little
this evening. Last night was a wild, mad night. Just
the time to saddle Goldfinder and Persimmon and
ride across the range! O Lord, how long? Pie-crust!
Pie-crust!!

Sat. Mar. 24. Well, I am a fool! I wish Jack was here.
He would help me out of my difficulties. No—if he
were here, I should not get into any.

April 15 Easter Sunday, 1900. Easter Sunday and
the sky is overcast; the wind is sobbing mournfully,
so different, O so different from that Easter so long
ago when—O fool, why, why, do you remember these
things when it is so much better you should forget?
You are happy now. You know you are. Let the dead
past bury its dead...Yes he is just away—I shall see
him again. The world is the better for his having
lived in it. Everything good that I am I owe to him.
Evening—Bert came up with Bill and the cart and
we went riding....

While the phantom Jack could be dismissed by a
visit from Bert or some other joyous occasion, Bert and
Lora's romance was forced to deal with a more tangible
reality—Papa.

Fri. Oct. 20, 1899. Pop is mad. He says if I can't go
anywhere without Bert following me, I shall stay at
home. He says I am too young (Ha-Ha!) to have
someone coming to see me regularly with serious
intentions....

Sat. Oct. 28, 1899. My <u>sixteenth</u> birthday ...Mamma and I went on reading and about 4 as I was reading "Five Little Peppers midway" Bert came to the door and I vanished. I intended to sit right there but I couldn't. I came out and he had <u>my</u> camera that he mustn't give me (<u>Darn</u>!) and gave me a box of candy. At 5 I started for the cows and I was strutting along like a "rediculous" turkey with my paws thrust deep into my pockets, whistling when here he came. He had taken leave of Mamma gone down the road till he was out of sight and then cut across. It was all the way he could get to speak to me at all and he walked over to where the cows were and clean back to the willows. Mamma thought he had gone straight to town and I didn't say anything.

Sun. Nov. 5, 1899. ...Nora came up on her new horse (she got from Fred Humphrey for $20) and wanted me to go riding so I caught Betie and we went. We met Pop and Dell hauling drift-wood before we got out of the brush....I met Jen and Mayme. They had come up to ride down with me....Bert came out and wanted to go....When we got through Jim Culleton's field here came Bert and he rode with us. We went over on the road and the gang were so far ahead we didn't catch them. We came home and Bert and I came through Dell's field. We walked down the little hill and we were talking and here came Pop! Heavens I was scared! <u>I skipped</u>! And he went right by me jumped off his horse and went to cussing Bert up to a peak. I skipped home and told Mamsie all about it and when Pop got home he never said a word to me. I wish he had. It was as much, no <u>more</u> my fault than Bert's.

Two days later Lora reported that "Pop is still on the warpath." However, Horace's objection to Lora's choice for a mate was quelled quietly as she noted on

Sunday, November 12, 1899, "This afternoon my
Yankee Doodle [cat] and I were reading and Bert came
up and interviewed Pop and then Mamma and I guess
its all right. I hope so, cause I wouldn't give Bert up for
anything and it will be nicer this way."

The school term began that November with an
unidentified teacher and Lora started, but apparently
her attendance was short-lived.

> *Sun. Nov. 26, 1899. I have to start to school tomor-*
> *row. (poor little cuss!) Bert was up this afternoon*
> *(Happy little cuss!).*

> *Mon. Dec. 4, 99. Went to school. Blame that teacher!*
> *Talk about fools. O yes! I know I hadn't ought to say*
> *it but I have thought it so what is the difference.*

After Papa and Mamma had come to an understanding with Bert, further formal education for Lora
seemed no longer a consideration. Yet, education was a
priority for the Nichols. During the year of Lora's
courtship and engagement to Bert Oldman, the *Herald*
reported in May that at the annual school meeting,
District #18, held at Doggett, the patrons voted to raise
by special tax $400.00 to be used for the construction of
a good school building. Lora's father Horace was a
member of the Board at this time and she commented:

> All my life either I or some member of my family has
> been a member of the school board, and *always* there
> were "wars and rumors of wars" over various contro-
> versial matters; at the time of which I write there
> had been bitter hard feelings, ever since the town
> was first established, between the "settlers" as the
> valley residents termed themselves and the group
> they looked upon as enemy "out-landers," the

despised Promoters of the new town-site. The chief bone of contention was the location of the school-house which all agreed should soon be built. The settlers favored a "center of the district" location and agreed among themselves on a grove of cottonwood trees about a half mile north of Riverside [Doggett], on the west side of the road, as a suitable location; the opposition group favored a "center of population" building-site. Many and bitter were the recriminations! My dad, who should, the settlers felt, have been on their side was called a turn-coat, a renegade, and other sneering epithets, because he felt that the school-house *should* be in a "center of population" spot. All this disapproval did not bother Dad, who was always one to stand by his convictions; Mother, Sis and I were deeply hurt....Dad used to say to us, "Don't *worry* so, girls. Hard words never broke any bones." This was small consolation to us.

(IR,73)

In addition to Horace's inflexible commitment to local education, were the facts that Sylvia's mother had been a teacher of languages before her marriage to the roaming George Washington Wilson, and that Lora's mother herself was attending the University of Colorado when she met Horace. The years in Colorado had been spent for the benefit of Lizzie and Lora's schooling and brother Guy Clifford had remained there at his grandparent's home in order to attend not only preparatory school, but also the University which David Nichols had helped establish. Lora and Lizzie, with their four full years of grammar school, their abbreviated sessions at the country school, and their intellectually lively home life, were as well educated as any young Wyoming ladies of the time.

Certainly Lora, at the time of her departure from formal schooling, was a self-directed learner. Nowhere is this more evident than in her enthusiastic pursuit of photography. In November of 1899, the Kodak, Bert's gift on the occasion of her sixteenth birthday, could now be hers as it was obvious that Pop thought better of him. She noted in the diary,

Sun. Nov. 19, 99. My dearest darling Bert was here this afternoon and he left my camera. He took my picture.

Wed. Nov. 22, 1899. Yesterday I took a picture of Mamma in the door and she took one of me and then we took Yankee outside and in the house and I took Nibs.

Thu. Nov. 23, 1899. I took Pop and Colonel's photo and Mum took me on Nibbs.

Lora's labels of some of her first pictures reflected the simplicity of her subjects:

The four "kids"—Jennie Ashley & Mayme Dunlap on two horses named "kid"; Maggie Nichols on Guy's pony "Bob" astride; Dad leading his bay stallion "Kodak" to water; Clella Brown on Klondike; Dell on General Crook afternoon going after broncs

Her entry on Monday, December 11, 1899, ended with, "My camera is the best fun." Papa solved a logistic problem even before Lora perceived it.

Fri. Dec. 22 / 99. Papa sent for me a developing outfit for Christmas so I can develope my own pictures.

+Tue. Jan. 9, 1900. Yesterday I got my developing outfit and last night I developed a roll of film....I printed two today. They are pretty good.

Mamma in the door

Within a few days of receiving her developing outfit, Lora was in the photography business.

*Sat. Jan. 13, 1900. Mrs. Dunlap wants me to come
down and take Dewey's picture.*

*+Thu. Mar. 15. I am to print 6 pictures for Mr. Ladd
& a dozen for Shorty.*

*Mon. March 19. Dell was up and got his pictures
and ordered half dozen of the other kind.*

Photograph taken by Mama
Lora in the door

*Tue. May 15, 1900. Went and took a picture of Mrs.
Vane's baby in his buggy this forenoon. Came home
and Mamma took me on Nibs and in the afternoon I
went over to the South Fork to take a picture of Lib's
pine tree, found it blown down and while I was con-
templating the result a man came along and
hemmed and hawed & hawed and wanted me to*

Photograph taken by Mama
Lora with Yankee

*take a picture of a hill across the river for him so I
did.*

*Wed. May 16. That man's name was J.S. Norvell (he
wrote it for me) and the hill he wanted taken was
the hill where the "Copperhead" Tunnel is to run. I
printed half a dozen for him and mailed them today.*

Papa harnessing Colonel

*Developed the film last night and took Mrs. Vane the
baby's picture today. She wants three of each. Got a
letter from Ira Wolfard and he wants one of himself
and two of Lee....*

*Tue. June 12. We washed this forenoon and this
afternoon I sewed on my quilt. Bert and I expect to
be married sometime next August if everything is
favorable. Dear old boy! I hope he will be as happy
as he thinks he will. Charley has leased our horses
for (I think) five years and he and Lib are going to
be here sometime.*

Bert, however, had one more obstacle, an unantici-
pated one. In June of 1900, Lora went on a pleasure
stay.

Carrie

Thu. June 14. Pop expects to go to Toga tomorrow and I will go to visit all my friends.

+Sat. June 16. "I am at Aunt Nan's now. Rode down with Pop and Mamma on the running gears and they went back today. This afternoon I went to the church Sociable and ate ice cream with the Bon Ton...

Cousins
Maggie, Guy Nichols, and Carrie Hinman

Sun. June 17. Last night we went to hear a lecture on temperance by Mrs. Bailey. She is just glorious! I never heard such talking in my life. She just stirred things. Then this morning at church she spoke again and at 8 P.M. to the women alone and organized a W.C.T.U. Got 31 members and I think she will probably get some more this evening. I think I'll join.

Mon. June 18. Well I did it. I'm a "white-ribboner" for the rest of my days. To join, one must sign a pledge never to use intoxicating liquors as a beverage, and pay fifty cents dues ever year. As this is the last half of this year we pay only 25 cents. But after this 50. There are 51 members in this Saratoga Union, 10 men as honorary members....

Family in the door
Uncle Platt, Carrie, Mamma, Aunt Nan, and Papa

In the saloons the teamsters, the eastern speculators, the double jack swingers, the newspaper men hired to expand the boom, the fledgling bankers gathered; these establishments were the exchange floors and the employment agencies of the early Mining District.

At one time at the very peak of Encampment's "Boom Days" there were in Encampment and Riverside a total of 16 bars, including those at the hotel and the several "Club Rooms"; three of these were in Riverside and the remaining 13 in Encampment. One is reminded of Alfred Henry Lewis's description of a pioneer town as, "a thriving little metropolis of ten houses and eleven saloons!" A church edifice was still non-existent but religious services were being held regularly at "Herald Hall" by a resident minister, H. Charles Dunsmore. [It was] known as "The Peoples' Church"....

(IR, 88)

Lora recorded an incident at Battle where Christian, civilizing influences met head on the temptation of drink.

Rev. John H. Murray added an interesting incident to his varied experience while conducting preaching services at Battle the other Sunday. He had invited one of the bartenders to come to church in the morning and the bartender in reply shook his hand and promised to be present. When the hour for the services came there were but two women present in addition to the party who had gone up from Grand Encampment with the minister. From the pulpit, Rev. Murray had a plain view of the saloon, which he watched for a few moments in hope of seeing the bartender start for the meeting. Suddenly a half dozen men rushed from the saloon in great confusion, and Rev. Murray said to himself that a fight must be on. After a short tussle the saloon door was locked and sixteen men walked over to the school house and sat down to hear the first sermon preached in Battle in a year. After the sermon, every one of these men walked up to the front and shaking hands with Rev. Murray thanked him for the words of cheer and gospel truth, in which they were reminded of the days gone by when they were back east in the land of churches and Christian influence. The bartender explained the confusion in front of the saloon by stating that when he announced that he would close up the place and go to church, two men refused to leave and he was compelled to throw them out, by force. The early training of many a young man engaged in the dealing out of strong drink is bound to crop out whenever there is an opportunity afforded. Rev. Murray's most successful work has been among the classes which the average preacher fails to reach.

(IR, 237)

Lora had heard about various neighbors and acquaintances "getting full," as she expressed it.

Sat. Jan. 7, 1899. Dell was up this evening. Just before he went home he was telling me about George Brown getting full. I wish he wouldn't.

Sun. Apr. 23, 1899. Well, Dell is at Doggett as full as a tick. It is a shame he won't leave whiskey alone when he knows he can. I don't know whether Bo drinks or not. I hope not. Why? What is it to me?

Now that they were betrothed, Bert's possible habits were of immense interest. Lora, as a full-of-fire initiate in the W.C.T.U., probably was unaware of the import of the saloon to Bert and his enterprises. With enthusiasm, she launched forth on temperance; he replied thoughtfully.

Fri. July 6. ...And do you know the darling boy promised me he would not drink any more. He did not, much but just took a bracer occasionally. O, I am so glad, so glad he promised to quit, because— because I don't know why but I am. O, I do love him so much and I can't express it, but I feel way down in my heart that I always shall. I'll "stand by him through thick and thin" as the saying is.

Jack Ledbetter photograph
Saloon at Battle in 1897

*Sun. July 15. ...He says "I think if it were possible
for me to love you more in one mood than another,
that is when you are serious." (I was speaking about
what a curse the liquor traffic was.) I am glad he
thinks that. Sometimes I feel serious when I think of
such things. Sometimes I want to tell him about our
W.C.T.U. and all the good it has done and is doing
and I know he would be interested in it. And he
says, "I know you have been through great trials,
and have come out with flying colors."*

In the thus morally charged atmosphere, as perceived by Lora before the wedding, she did elicit from
Bert a confession and a vow.

Sun. Aug. 19, 1900. ...[Cousin] Maggie came on up with me. She had to go to the livery stable after a piece of casting Uncle Ez had sent for, for the mower. Nobody was there but we finally hunted Darrel up and he saw about it. While Maggie was talking to him, Bert came across the street and spoke to me. He had just said, "I bummed last night," and was looking pretty serious when Maggie called me to go down to the Rankin Hotel with her to see about the casting. She went on home then and I came on up towards the road home, hoping I would see Bert for I wanted him to tell me how he had "bummed." Sure enough as I was going by the Post Office, he came out and walked up the road with me. And he said he had gambled the night before, after he went down from here. O, I felt terrible about it for a few minutes and then I managed to collect my wits and say something. He promised, though that he would never do it again, and I know he won't for he wouldn't break a promise.

I WISH I WAS A YELLOW DOG

IF BERT MADE CONCESSIONS in promising to discard his minor vices—of either "a bracer" or a small, occasional wager—he also demanded some concessions from Lora. Shortly before the wedding, Bert and some of the boys were to be gone overnight while fighting a timber fire up the canyon.

> *Thu. Aug. 16, 1900. Bert said he didn't want me to go to the dance tomorrow night so I am not going.*

Lora acquiesced but Bert's demand on a more personal topic drew her first fire at her intended.

> *+Thu. Sept. 13. Yesterday, just after dinner, Mr. and Mrs. Baggott drove up, much to our surprise. And shortly afterward while I was in my room hating myself and all the world, Bert came. He wanted to borrow Nibs to go and get his horse to put in our pasture. I went over with him to catch him and he said a few things about my divided skirt. I felt pretty sore about it all day today as well as yesterday afternoon but I guess I am ready to take a reasonable view of it now. He went on and got his horse*

and went riding up the canyon. He has entirely too
sharp a pair of eyes. He knew I had been crying,
when he got back with his horse....

+Sat. Sept. 15. Yesterday morning Mum and I
sewed....Bert was up in the evening. O dear! I <u>hate</u> to
have that skirt lengthened! But I must. Bert won't
<u>insist</u> on my having lengthened, he is like the little
boy who gave his little brother his choice of two
apples: the little one or none. I can either have that
skirt fixed or have him look like anger personified
every time he sees me with it on.

On September 21, 1900, Lora told Diary, "My things
came last night and are all satisfactory. The wedding
dress is 'super' and the tan shoes are the swellest
things you ever saw."

++ Mon. Oct. 1, 1900. ...Yesterday Bert was up and
spent the afternoon and evening. He says, "Only two
more Sundays and I'll come up and see you and
then you'll be my little wife." Just think! Only two
weeks! It fairly scares me. I want to do just as he
wants me to but I'm so dreadfully head-strong....

Mon. Oct. 15, 1900. My wedding day. How strange
that seems. Cousin Maggie stayed up here last night.
She brought me a lovely plate glass mirror with an
Indian or some sort of beast holding it up. I guess
Uncle Platt will stay. Bert was up last night. Lizzie
gave me a doll pincushion dressed in cerise silk with
white lace and green ribbon. It is 10.45 now. Maggie
and I have loafed around on the bed for about an
hour, and I split up a couple rounds of wood and
that is about all I have done today so far. This after-
noon I must catch Colonel and put him in the barn.

+++++Sun. Oct. 21. Well, here we are again. We will have been married a week tomorrow and strange to say, I don't regret it. Monday, just after we had finished dinner Aunt Nan and Carrie came. Well, we fooled around until time to dress me. They got me all fixed up in time and I went out and Bert and I walked in and took our places and the Reverend Norvell got up and commenced operations and then I began to shake. I got over it in a minute and was alright. We ate our "wedding supper" and after a while Bert and I departed, amid showers of good wishes....They gave us our "charavarie" the next night. Mrs. Heather finally got my photos done and I rigged up a couple and a piece of wedding cake for Cliff. Bert is going into the hills to work for a few days and I am going back home—no—not home— this is home now.

Wednesday, Nov. 7. 10:45 A.M. Bert rode Nibs up into the hills today. In the Oct. 19th "Herald" our wedding notice is in.

Mr. A.H. Oldman and Miss Lora Nichols were united in marriage at the home of the bride's parents Mr. and Mrs. H.A. Nichols, Monday evening, Rev J.S. Norvell officiating. The wedding was a quiet affair, only a few relatives being present. The young couple are both well known and highly respected and have the best wishes of a large circle of friends. Mr. and Mrs. Oldman are now keeping house in their residence on Heizer Avenue.

Bert don't like it. He says its "bum."...

The log homestead house built by Papa in the late 1880s, the house of the settler gatherings before the coming of Grand Encampment City, the house of Lora and Lizzie's coming of age, now had been the setting of

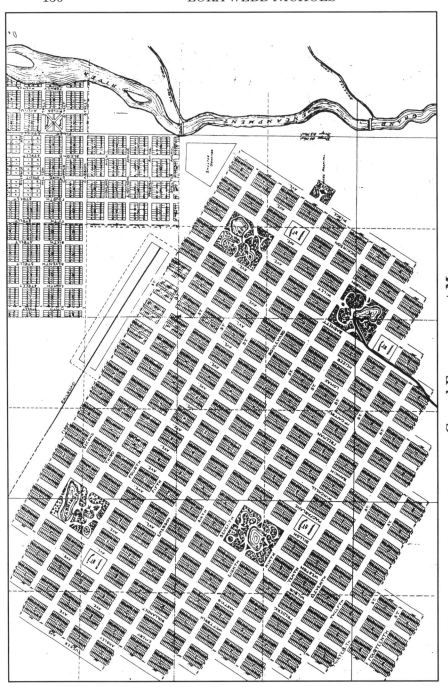

Grand Encampment Map

Early Construction in the Boomtown
Frank Lordier is at the drugstore with Bert's dog, Duke.

the weddings of both girls. Lora reported that the dear old homestead house was beginning to decay and Papa had begun the building of a new house; at the time of Lora's wedding, the structure made a brave showing of several logs high, the logs cut in the hills and brought to the site by Charley. The new home at Willow Glen was to be an ambitious two stories high in striking contrast to the original ground-hugging homestead house. Lora, inclined to name every inanimate thing, rechristened the older homestead house "Glen Cottage" in deference to its smaller size.

The housing shortage and the lack of building materials posed a dilemma to many people attracted to the boom city of Grand Encampment. Papa, however

Success!
Lordier Drug, constructed in 1901

(with his log construction) and Charley (his son-in-law, helper, and hauler) were not concerned with those issues.

Most of those early houses were built of "green" lumber, freshly sawed. Nobody had time to wait for lumber to "season!" This green lumber shrank as it dried and boards that had been nailed touching each other, all of a sudden had mighty cracks between them. The shrinking lumber also loosened the nails, and the upkeep problem was a real one. I well remember my own first home in Encampment, which was typical of all; my husband, Bert Oldman, came into the camp the winter of 1897-8 and worked on the development of several groups of claims owned by the Colorado

Springs promoters. The town-site companies were at that time giving to any local resident who would promise to erect a house on it one of the residence lots as listed on the Town Plat. These lots were 25 x 115 and as a rule the men building on them bought another lot, in order as they said to have "room enough to change my mind." Bert put up a two room house where he "batched" very comfortably; before we were married, in October 1900, he built on a ten foot kitchen at the back. This was, in its original state a single board wall, made of green lumber. The boards, which were 12 inches wide, were nailed on the studding in a vertical position; pretty soon they began to shrink and as the cracks appeared, Bert nailed battens over them. So far, so good; but the wide boards continued to shrink and split the battens and it was then found necessary to make a more substantial wall which was accomplished with the aid of heavy building paper, applied over the original boards and an additional course of boards on top of the paper, so that eventually we had a wall that kept the cold out quite efficiently. Several of my young friends who had recently married, were living in similar houses and we brides had a lot of fun laughing over our difficulties. One girl's husband told her that when the cracks got wider than the boards he would put on another course. One thing we all enjoyed was the clean tangy smell of those pitchy pine boards.

(IR,69)

The Grand Encampment that greeted Lora as a young bride was far different from the "embryo town" with "one log cabin and a few tents...with the Stars and Stripes flying over the company office" that had greeted the Nichols on May 20, 1897. Lora quotes an article from the April 19, 1901, *Grand Encampment Herald*

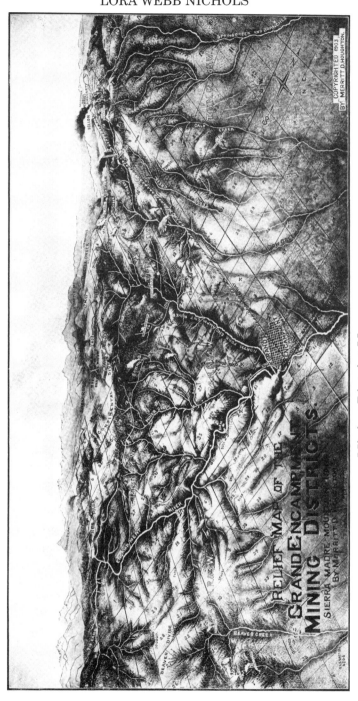

Mining District Map

Photographer unknown

Dillon Hotel

touting, with at least essential truth, the wonders of the city.

Grand Encampment in its growth, the number and speedy development of its mines, the influx of people to the town and surrounding copper and gold fields, is not unlike the condition of things which characterized the early days of Cripple Creek.

So rapid has been the transformation from nothing—from a bleak and almost uninhabited country to a district embracing numerous towns, embryo settlements and mining camps, that we can scarcely realize the facts as they today exist. And yet these changes have occurred within the brief period of three years, in which time fully three thousand people have gathered here from almost every quarter of the Union.

Photographer unknown
Rawlins Stage at the Ferris Mercantile Company in Dillon

The gold fever has always been contagious, and men have been smitten with it in all lands and in all ages. In this instance, however, the disease proves to be of a different type, as the ores in this district are almost wholly a copper product.

Grand Encampment is the center of the greatest copper district that has been discovered in the west, and from the present indications it may develope into the richest mining camp of the kind in the entire country.

The town is situated at the junction of the North and South forks of the Grand Encampment rivers.

There followed a long list of businesses and public services offered by the town. Among them were: 1 bank

Photographer unknown
Scribner Stage at Encampment

with $28,000 deposit, 1 newspaper, 3 general stores, 2 dry goods establishments, 1 bakery, 2 meat markets, 2 lodging houses, 2 blacksmith shops, 2 livery stables, 1 assay office, 3 physicians, 2 lawyers, 2 barber shops, 1 brick yard, and 2 U.S. Deputy Mineral surveyors. The Encampment Post Office had 600 patrons.

The town is connected by daily stages with Collins, Saratoga, Battle, Fort Steele, and Walcott....

Supplementing its advantages as a mining center Grand Encampment possesses a healthful and invigorating climate, picturesque scenery, fine fishing and good hunting grounds.

Unlike Cripple Creek and Leadville the altitude here is from two to three thousand feet lower, hence the climate is more congenial in summer and less rigorous in winter.

Looking to the near future, the article declared:

Nine new houses are being erected, and during the coming summer building will go rapidly forward. Among those being constructed is a two story hotel (annex to the Bohn House) which will contain 31 rooms and be equipped with many modern conveniences. The town will soon have an electric light and water plant, the water being drawn from the Encampment River, water pure, cold and excellent.

(GEH/IR, 81–4)

Lora was well acquainted with Grand Encampment when Bert took her, on their wedding day, to his little frame house. Many of Lora's best friends, Belle and Edna Wilcox and Jenny Ashley, Carl's sister, were among the young brides that shared the boomtown joys and blues with Lora. Upon Lora's arrival, Bert's bachelor establishment became "Cosy" Cottage. With the ranch within walking distance, Lora carried pieces of her old life to her new, never making the transfer complete.

Friday, Nov. 16. ...I went up to the ranch this morning and found Yankee and brought him down. He was badly scared as you may well suppose and howled most of the way though he only fought and scratched twice. He couldn't do any harm of course for I had him in a "gunny-bag." He settled down as peacefully as anyone's cat once he got here and seems to be quite contented. I brought down a cake recipe and a glass of jelly too and this afternoon I made a cake. It wasn't a failure, strange to say...

Photographer unknown
Girls on Nibbs
Lora, Jenny, and Maggie

+Wed. Jan. 23. Yesterday Bert worked and I ironed, baked bread and darned socks all my spare minutes. Today Bert felt bum so I got up and got breakfast and then called him. He felt better after a while and concluded to go to work so I left everything and went with him as far as Mamma's and stayed all day. Brought Birdy down tonight when we came....

In a time given to overzealous modesty and reticence about the human body, Lora's frank, offhand mention of the physical aspect of her marriage, even to Diary, showed proof of her innocence and free spirit.

*Monday, October 22. It seems like so many days that
I have been without "thee, my diry" that I must have
another little talk with you. Bert is just a <u>perfect</u>
husband and having to ——— you know what isn't
as bad as I thought it would be. O, I forgot to mention that on Monday evening Jen and Mayme each
brought me a wedding present. Jen brought a silver
nut-cracker and six picks and Mayme brought one of
those blue "plate" card receivers with a pink ribbon
around the edge. <u>My</u> I was pleased! ...*

*Tuesday, Oct. 30. 1900. Yesterday afternoon it
snowed and there was some snow on the ground this
morning and it has been quite cold today. Last night
when I went to go to bed, it seemed so familiar to be
going to bed in my own little room but I just didn't
know how to go to sleep without Bert. I always sleep
on his arm and he lets me have the front of his shirt
unbuttoned and put my face on his bare breast and
it's so nice to have someone you <u>like</u> to sleep with
you. You know sometimes when I used to have to
sleep with someone I didn't like, it used to make me
<u>so</u> mad. O, Dear! ...*

*+Mon. Jan. 14. ...After a while Bert went up town
and when he came back he walked in, looking rather
sheepish and said, "I don't know what you'll do to
me." I asked why and he said he had asked three
people down to supper....I was surprised and I must
confess not very much pleased. I had been crosser
than two sticks all day....Well, they came alright and
we had a regular jollification....They went home
about half past nine and Bert read me a chapter of
"A Yankee from the West" he had been reading aloud
and we went to bed and then—let us draw the curtain of charity over the scene!*

A late period set her upon an emotionally charged speculation that she might be pregnant.

Monday, Nov. 2. I am afraid there is rather a strong prospect of the triplets. It doesn't please me much but I don't have to die just to verify a doctors word. I just won't that's all there is to it.

Mon. Jan. 21, 1901. I haven't come around yet and I guess my little red-headed boy thought the weather was so nice he had better start on his long journey.

In subsequent entries her main concern was her own health and Bert's possible reaction to the pregnancy. The "doctor" and "Dr. May" she alluded to perhaps was a physician in Boulder; Lora seemed to have an undefined heart condition during her youth.

Thu. Jan. 24. ...The blues took possessions of me today. This morning at breakfast I talked so moodily Bert came around and knelt beside my chair, put his arms around me laid his face against my breast and looked up at me in such a sorrowful puzzled way I could hardly keep from crying. In fact I believe I did a little bit, when I got my face hidden on his shoulder. I haven't quite recovered my equanimity yet, and all on account of my little red-headed boy. O, if only I knew whether Dr. May was right. I want my little baby and I know now that Bert wants him too. The other evening we were discussing him and Bert said, "I would like one little baby to love." O Bert, I would like one too but if I should have to go away and leave you—O I can't breathe tonight. Bert nearly broke my heart this morning—and I don't think he meant—I think he loves me, if he didn't I think I should want to die but he said if he had lived in the same house with me for two years, he doesn't think

*he would have married me. If he had known how
that remark was going to hurt me he wouldn't have
made it. I love him so Perhaps this bit of verse may
express my feelings for me—I can't.*

I do not ask thee what thou art.
Nor what thy life in great or small.
Thou art, I know what all my heart,
Must beat or break for—that is all.

*Fri. Jan. 25, 1901. ...He [Bert] said, about the baby,
"Well, I'm sorry this happened quite so soon." I suppose he isn't quite ready to get rid of me yet, but perhaps he will be by the time the baby comes. Even
though I live; this sounds cruel and unnatural I
know; but I hope and pray that my baby will die
before it is a year old. O God—not for my sake but
for its own. Bert went to work today and I ought to
be busy too, I have several things to do so I will dismiss the subject and go to work But let me say there
is pleasure for me, even in pain if he caused it.*

*Tue. Jan. 29. ...I came around today so there wasn't
any little red-headed boy after all.*

As a bride, Lora could not carry to the marriage her
sense of privacy and self-determination, both so fos-
tered in the Nichols' homestead. As with her rebellion
against lengthening her divided skirt because Bert
wished it, Lora's wrath often was recorded in Diary
and, through this writing process, was extinguished
and never wielded against Bert. The occasion was a
projected trip to see Lizzie, now staying in Saratoga
while Charley was hauling from the coal bank. Lora's
response even condemned her dear mamma for supporting Bert's opinion, the only lines in the entire diary
to voice anger at her mother.

Sat. Dec. 1. ...Bert has gone over town now. I want to go to Toga and make Lib a visit but Bert don't want me to go alone (Hang it all and so I can't ride Nibs down like I had set my heart on doing). Great guns and ammunition! I wish I was a yellow dog. I could go then without someone hanging over me like cut glass. I'd honestly rather not go than to go with someone. O but it does grate on me but I won't be such an idiot O! O!! ...Let me out! I try not to act mad about it and I endeavor not to scratch out Bert's or Mamma's eyes when they say "Yes, I think it would be best; it isn't quite safe for you to go so far alone." O Lord! Well, I'm mad, I'm mad enough to kill somebody, and I know I ought not to be. O yes indeed, I know all about it but that doesn't prevent my feeling as though I'd like to go clear to San Francisco, alone. Gee Whiz! What am I alive for any-way.

Wed. Dec. 5. Charley and I had a good trip yester-day. I wore his big blanket-lined, duck overcoat and had a horse blanket over my knees and around my feet. We discussed nearly everything under the sun and were speaking about liking Wyoming and Charley said, "Well it maybe ain't as nice as south-ern California but a poor man can't float along on flowery beds of ease all the time." Lizzie was much surprised and equally delighted...Wrote to Bert and Mamma today and mailed the letter. I wore Lizzie's new cow-boy hat over to town....

Lora found that Bert didn't object so much either to her going or to the destination as he did to her plan of traveling alone on Nibs. At Saratoga Lora's days and evenings with Lizzie were spent in a flurry of visiting old friends and new, singing while Lizzie played her fid-dle, pulling taffy at the neighbors, going "up town."

Judging from the amount of space devoted to it in the
diary, Lora's bath at the remodeled Saratoga spa was
an event in the life of this girl who had never experienced the joy of indoor plumbing.

*Sat. Dec. 8. ...We went over to the Hot Springs Hotel
and took a "barf" [bath]. They have things fixed up
pretty nice now, that is, compared with what they
were. There used to be a little, one-horse house, three
bath rooms with wooden bath tubs, having a broad
strap, on which to rest your head. They pumped your
bath as you wanted it and when the tub got full you
rapped on the window for him to stop pumping. Now
they have a fine, large two-story bath-house, adjoining the Hotel and all the upper story is the Ladies
bathrooms. They have a nice waiting room with
wash basin and hot & cold water faucets, heater, etc.
The bath tubs are porcelain lined and there is hot &
cold water and a shower bath, full length window
with shade and sash curtain and a chunk of carpet
to stand on and a chair to sit on.*

LESSON IN MINING

LORA'S INCUBUS, however, was not her perception of
Bert's domination nor was it her own strong will. It
came from an unexpected source. During the courtship,
when Mrs. Bailey (in Saratoga) inspired her to become
"a white ribboner," Lora was concerned about Bert's
patronizing the numerous saloons of the Mining
District. As Grand Encampment moved beyond the
first blasts of the boom, a new, more proper institution
provided a gentlemen's meeting place—both for pleasure and for business. The lodges and clubs were central to Grand Encampment's burgeoning social life.
They brought together the folks of the mining camps
and those of the countryside. Many an immigrant
drawn to the mining or agricultural riches of the valley
was initiated into the English language and the
American way, or at least the Wyoming way, through
lodge ritual and fellowship. Lora's papa and Bert both
joined. In 1900 "The Lodge Directory began to appear
in the paper; Encampment Lodge AF and AM, White
Cloud Tribe #10, IORM and Menzie Camp # 5927 MWA
being the only ones represented" (GEH/IR, 88).

Bert Oldman photograph
Lodge
Charter Members of the IOOF

Wednesday. Nov. 7, 1900. 8.15 P.M. Bert has gone to lodge and I am keeping house all by my lonesome.

Thursday. Nov. 8. 4.30 P.M. Bert was out to lodge last night until 1.30 this morning so we weren't up very early.

+Sat. Nov. 10. Bert has gone to the Redman Lodge again....Wednesday night and Thursday night they organized and tonight is their first regular meeting. Papa is the Great Sachem....

Saturday, November 24. It seems to me that old Lodge keeps him up town a good deal when I want him down here with me.

Nov. 29, Thanksgiving Day 1900. Last night Bert came down from the hills and we came on down home and stayed overnight. This morning we fooled around getting things straightened out and Bert went over town to get shaved, found the Barber Shop shut and was obliged to shave himself....About 5 Bert and I started for home. He has gone up town to see if he got any mail and pretty soon we will start for the "Redman Ball." (N.B. I don't admire Redman balls myself.) Got a letter from Lib last night.

Tue. Jan. 8. 1901. Bert joined the Woodmen last night and was out till 12. This morning he went to work clear up on Finley Hill. I washed.

Sat. Jan. 12. It blew again this morning so Bert didn't go to work. He built a cupboard in the corner of the kitchen for me to keep odd traps in....My old demon "rose from the dead" yesterday and I've been having it hot and heavy with him ever since. It is evening and Bert is up town. He goes up town every evening and gets back very seldom before nine and often not until half past ten. I haven't any room to kick of course but—O bow-wow—little dog. I wish my guardian angel could come down and talk to me this evening....I feel like crying. Guess I will. No, I mustn't for Bert would come home and know I had been crying and then he would want to know the reason. Of course I wouldn't tell him. O, me! What a goose I am to be sure—but—I can't help it—O, Bert, Bert! My darling. Well—I leaned forward onto this book with my eyes full of tears—ready, I suppose, to drop a "sentimental tear upon the page" —and doubtless would have done so had I not looked up at the glass opposite me and burst out laughing at the lugubrious countenance that confronted me. I will not cry! I won't do it. I'll—I'll get Mother Goose and read it first. 10 P.M. Bert got back about 8 with a

Cosy Cottage in the Rough

package from mother....This package contained the cups & saucers (lovely Chinese ones) creamer and sugar bowl (little cute ones awful nice) and a little Chinese cup and saucer she had sent me, a lot of ribbons all nice ones, of every color, a set of side & front combs, three nice petticoats, a bee-u-tiful black dress trimmed in canary yellow. It was given her & cost $3.50 a yard when new....Wasn't that nice? But dear me, She does too much for us. Bert had to go to Lodge and hasn't got back yet.

Using her diary to ascend to the melodramatic and then dismiss the case had become typical for Lora. Upon numerous occasions, she threatened "Diary" with burning, but it had, in truth, become her confidante, the recipient of her wrath and her elation, her every

Corner, with Daybed

mood recorded in lively, fresh prose. Lora, at eighteen with four years of her life recorded in the assorted diaries, began to philosophize about her expanding self-portrait.

Sat. Feb. 23. ...My diary—I wonder what kind of an estimate of my character any one reading these pages would form. A pretty correct one? No—I don't think so. It is all so jumbled up—I have written in some of my worst moods—for it is then that I want you—my diary, and in very—very few good ones. Very inconsistent, silly and superficial.

Mon. May 13. ...Isn't it funny how conceited and self-important sounding a diary is? It is I—I—I— from beginning to end. Perhaps if I didn't think myself such a high muck-a-muck, it wouldn't sound

Interior, with Rocker and Stove

*so. But I know I don't amount to much. I don't cut
much figure. I can't seem to do any good in the
world—my own little world and in point of fact it
seems to me I'm rather an encumbrance on the face
of the earth. Nevertheless I'm here and will have to
keep pegging away trying to make myself useful.
Perhaps I'd succeed better if I were not so selfish and
always looking out for number one. O, ring off!
Confound that milk-man I wish he'd hurry. I'm tired
and I want to go to bed.*

By the spring of 1901, Lora's adamant commitment
to written self-expression was complemented by her
new allegiance to the visual record. Her Kodak had
become part of Lora's traveling outfit. After her marriage to Bert, Lora documented both the interior and

Bert, in Rocker

exterior of "Cosy Cottage," and all the subsequent improvements made by Bert.

++ *Tue. Feb. 19. This morning I took a couple of time exposures of our "drawing room" I don't know whether they'll be good or not.*

She photographed Duke by the doorstep and Bert in the new rocker. After months of enthusiastic picture taking, Lora discovered Bert now had misgivings about Lora and the Kodak.

Sat. Apr. 27. 1901. 7.45. P.M. This morning Bert Dunlap brought a note to Mum and me from Mrs. Dunlap informing us that they were going to give the Redmen another little "impromptu lunch" so we are going to that. This morning we made cakes for it

Cosy Cottage, Complete

*and this afternoon I went up to Lib's. [At] about four,
Bert came up the road seeking me. He was early and
I wasn't expecting him yet. I have been anticipating
this "doin's" all day. But this evening Bert and I
were talking and he asked me if I was broke and I
told him "Yes" because I had sent all my money to
Montgomery Ward & Co. and he asked me what for;
I told him (It was mounts and printing-paper) and
he said, "Are you going to give them all away?" I
said if I couldn't give them away then they weren't
mine and then he said I'd keep him broke buying
photographic materials! I supposed when he gave
me money that it was to buy whatever I wanted to
with and if it isn't I don't want any—so there. And
besides I don't believe I have spent more than $2.00
for photographic materials since we have been mar-*

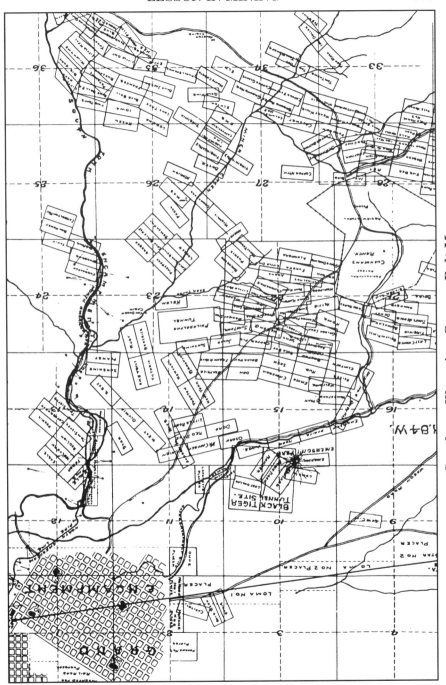

Southern Wyoming Copper Belt Map

Showing mining claims near Grand Encampment City

*ried that I didn't <u>earn</u> my own self with the camera.
If he expected me to save that money to buy clothes
and such things with he should have <u>said</u> so and
not have told me it was to "<u>blow.</u>" Oh I think it was
<u>cruel</u> of him to say that. God knows <u>I</u> don't enjoy
being dependent on him for every cent I have. And I
didn't mean to waste it foolishly. Oh this all looks
very silly—doesn't it? Quite too silly to tell anyone
but you—diary mine. Oh dear, oh dear. I don't want
to go to that supper <u>at all</u> now, I want to stay at
home so I can cry.*

Lesson in Mining

A lode is a streak, as sure as you're born,
A dip is a pitch of the same.
A big bunch of rock, that spoils the pay shoot,
Is called a horse in the vein.

A hanging wall's the top, you know,
Or roof, of leads in place.
The foot-walls just the floor of them,
Or the bottom, bed, or base.

An incline shaft is one that's sunk,
Down on the leads own pitch,
A straight one just don't seem to care,
'Bout strikin' ore that's rich.

A cross-cut runs to tap the vein
From a point that's picked as best.
A tunnel's about the same old thing,
So we'll let that subject rest.

A drift is a tunnel that follows a lead
Not down, but in on a level.
A stope's a hole where ore was mined,
Now don't that beat the devil?

A winze is a sort of shaft, you see,
That starts from a level below,
And why they picked that name for it
Is more, my friend, than I know.

A raise is made to connect two levels
Or to strike the shoot overhead.
And the face of a drift is the end of the thing,
And so we'll say, enough said.
                    Quoted by Lora—Diary +Mon. Apr. 4, 1904

Bert Oldman was the epitome of the peripatetic prospector, speculator, miner; he labored in almost every possible capacity that the Grand Encampment Mining District offered. Bert did locate some claims of his own. However, for day-to-day existence, he, and then Lora too, were dependent upon an incoming paycheck from other sources. This dependency, first, upon Mr. Bohrer and the Colorado Springs investors and later upon various other employers, made Bert's life precarious. Often, even in the glory of the boom, there were doldrums and no jobs for him at all.

Sat. Feb. 16, 1901. My poor darling has the blues dreadfully, You know he has been out of work for some time and he can't get a job and then Mr. Bohrer not sending him the last money on that Miner Creek work, leaves him in rather a fix.

Tuesday March 19, 1901. Bert was going to work but it was still storming so he didn't and this afternoon he was down town and the man he was going to work for had gone and taken someone else. Wasn't that a great way to do?

Jack Ledbetter photograph
Men at the Portland Tunnel

Although the social life offered by the new city of Grand Encampment altered Lora's adolescence, before her marriage she was on the periphery of the mining activity that had prompted the town's establishment. Uncle Platt Hinman, Aunt Nan's husband and Carrie's father, had a gold claim, the Blue Belle, and the Nichols

Jack Ledbetter photograph
Ore Car Panorama

often visited there. Looking from her window in the homestead house, she watched the promenade of teamsters, horsemen, and foot travelers—all on their way to possible glory holes the hills. In the spring of 1900 a vortex of activity came much closer. While *The Grand Encampment Herald* applauded claims near the city, Lora's papa had his own response.

> "The foot-hills about a mile west of town are again attracting prospectors and several promising discoveries have been made within the past month. C A Finley, A A Sherrod and A W Anding have all located

Jack Ledbetter photograph
Camp at Columbine

claims with veins in place and rich surface showings and are doing extensive prospecting on the ground. Good float has frequently been found in that locality but prospectors have generally passed it by for higher ground. Systematic work will now be done and it would not be surprising if something good were found." It was during this rush of springtime prospecting that Dad found a "location stake" in the middle of a potato patch he had planted on the west side of the creek. He considered that the joke of a lifetime, and told all his friends about it, saying, "If he can develope a copper mine in my potato patch, I'll sure get out of his way!"

(GEH/IR 75)

Jack Ledbetter photograph
Prospector

In her marriage to Bert, Lora learned not only her "Lesson in Mining," but also her lessons in being a very young wife—first in the scamper and then in the slack of the Grand Encampment Mining District. Caught in the almost excessive convivial swirl of the village, too little time remained for her beloved solitary pursuits, straining her sociability. During her introduction to life in Grand Encampment, she wrote:

Thu. May 17. 1900. ...Now this is going to sound foolish but I am just positively sick tonight from the mental strain I've been up to all day. O, I hate "social intercourse" I hate it! O, I don't know what makes me so bad, so unreasonable. I guess God

made me for an experiment and a dismal failure I
am. He will never make another after that pattern.
But I'll conquer. I will—I am, why I've got so I can
stand it to listen to someone talk for a whole day
and can say "No?" "Indeed?" "Now isn't that nice?"
"Now that's just what I've always thought." Just
when I should, with the proper simper and all. O,
I'm improving (?) I am.

During the first four years of her marriage, Lora experienced a dozen changes of household including numerous brief stays at the ranch and in mining cabins. The fortunes of the Oldmans depended upon the good luck of Bert. As surely as she tacked carpet down and pulled it up, she dutifully christened each domicile—no matter the length of her stay. Often too, she recorded the stay with her ever-present Kodak. Bert and Lora's first venture from "Cosy Cottage," their honeymoon home, occurred the next spring when Bert hired on to work on a tunnel for Mr. Bryne. They rented Cosy Cottage to the Bentleys.

Saturday, Mar. 30, 1901. We had quite a nice time at
the dance. Came home at midnight, and today I
have been packing up some things preparatory to
leaving our dear darling home. It is quite breaking
my heart to leave it and I don't know when we will
come back; perhaps not at all. Bert and the carpen-
ter are finishing the other bedroom. Mrs. & Miss
Bentley were up to see the house for a few min-
utes....Tomorrow Bert is going to help me pack the
rest of our things and Monday he is going to work.

Sunday, Mar. 31. Well, we finished packing up our
things today and moved. Bentleys came and Mr. B.
hauled our things up to Mamma's....I was cross as
two sticks all day and felt like destruction but I feel

Jack Ledbetter photograph
Woodpile at the Doane Rambler

*better since I saw my Mummy. Well, you see with try-
ing to pack things without knowing how and you
know if there is a wrong way to do a thing that is
surely the way I would do it. I got things all
"momoxed" and Bert had to pack his trunk over
again and I know he was out of patience with me for
being such a goose but I did my best.*

*Camp Winona, +++ Sun. Apr. 7, 1901. On Thursday
I went to Charley's and stayed all day. A blamed
chump from Michigan, one of Prof. Burt's friends,
who had been working up with Bryan (or rather his
name is Bryne) came up to the door and said he was
lost. Imagine it! He came straight down the canyon,
cut through Pop's field and when he struck the lane,
turned the wrong way and went up Finley Hill clear
to the top and had to retrace his steps. He hadn't the*

faintest idea where he was and he wasn't a mile from town. I developed a roll of film in the evening. Friday, Lib and I went to town after some things and over to see Mrs. Bryne. Found them packing up to go up in the hills so I "hiked" back quick and got my things so I could go up with them....We had quite a pleasant trip. Mr. Bryne had to transfer the load from the wagon to the sled and Mrs. Bryne & I walked quite a ways over a sliding place. We didn't get here until about 8. Mrs. B. and I stopped at the Victor cabin where Mrs. Bob Foyle is staying only a little ways from us until Bert and Mr. Bryne and Mike Kayllier got unloaded and some fires built at our cabin. On Saturday we straightened around some and Mr. B went back after some more things. Today is Sunday and Easter too. Mr. B. brought the rest of the things. Bert is working at boarding the inside of the cabin. It wasn't done.

Mon. Apr. 8, 5.30 P.M. It is snowing; has been all day. Bert went to work the night shift tonight with Perry Foyle but we went down to see "our neighbors" a few minutes ago (Bert and I) and Perry says, "Not on your tintype." He and his wife and baby just got here today and the wagon is stuck down the road about a quarter of a mile with their stuff.

Tue. Apr. 9. I went for a walk today. Had a nice time though I broke into the snow at a great rate. The snow is about three feet as a rule. Bert isn't suited. I am afraid he will leave soon.

Wed. Apr. 10. Bert went to town today to see what he could see. I took a couple of pictures of the cabin this morning from between the cabin and the creek. This is the way the cabin is situated.

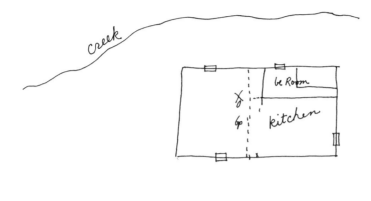

I don't know whether or not Bert will stay here much longer. I like it very much, only of course, when I feel he is discontented I can't be happy.

Thu. Apr. 11. Well—I got called down today. And about not doing my share of the work too. The worst of it is Mrs. B. had right on her side. The only excuse I could have offered (I offered none) was utterly inadequate to the occasion. That was this morning and it is 5 P.M. now and everything has resumed its accustomed proportions. Even my temper. Bert is to work night shift tonight and is gone now. That will bring him home about 1.30 in the morning. So he will get quite a bit of sleep. Last night when Bert came home he brought me some nice candy, dates and peanuts. He is a darling Love of a boy.

Fri. Apr. 12. Well, Bert worked night shift and tried to sleep today but Tommy "raised H——l and put a prop under it," as Grandpa used to say. This after-noon after he got up—he and I went down to see Perry Foyle. They have a tent boarded up to live in and are fixed quite comfortably. I took two pictures

*of "scenery" today; right up the creek a little way
from the cabin.*

*Sat. Apr. 13. 9 P.M. Well things came to a crisis. Last
night Bert went to work and Mr. Bryne got back
from town about 9 and a little after in walked Bert.
He had worked a half shift and quit because rocks
kept falling from the top of the tunnel and one hit
him on the head. He said he wasn't going to stay
and risk his life. Mr. Bryne wasn't pleased. This
morning we packed our stuff so Mr. Bryne could
bring it down Monday and taking our hand satchel
and Kodak, "we hit the pike" and arrived at the
ranch about noon. Lib and Charley had been to dinner at Dell's and spent most of the afternoon here.
Bert and Pop have gone to Lodge.*

After Bert and Lora escaped from "Camp Winona,"
Bert worked briefly on the construction of the new
smelter above Riverside (lately Doggett). Throughout
its years of operation, the smelter was to provide Bert
an occasional job. In *I Remember,* Lora quoted the
Herald to document the extent of the copper boom and
the history of the smelter.

In January 1900 there were filed in the office of the
Secretary of State at Cheyenne, articles of incorpora-
tion for three companies which played a most important part in the development of Grand Encampment:
the Boston–Wyoming Smelter Power and Light
Company, the Frambaugh Waterworks Company and
the Emerson Electric Light Co.

GEH/IR, 60

The month of April saw continued increase in buildings erected in town, new businesses established,
and new mining properties going into production.

The price of copper continued to rise, being quoted in the Herald at this time as follows: "COPPER MAR-KET TODAY—Strong at $17.25, Brokers' price $17.50....The Ferris–Haggarty is at present the largest shipper, the value of the ore reaching over $400,000 since the spring of 1899." Then follow the Kurtz–Chatterton, Rambler, Charter Oak, Coldwater, Union Syndicate, Hercules, Haskins, Elk Mountain, Copper Belt, Comstock, Cox...and hundreds of others which are now in initial stages of development.

(GEH/IR, 67)

The first pictures of the Smelter under construction appeared in the paper Feb. 22, 1901 showing the frame-work of the ore bins, of which there were twelve each with a capacity of one hundred tons. Another picture showed a portion of the smelter building and the frame work of the engine room. Machinery for the smelter was arriving and it was expected to be in operation by May 1st.

(IR, 81)

Bert obviously viewed his first smelter position as temporary.

Mon. May 13. He is very tired tonight but has gone up town to "see a man."

Tue. May 14, 1901. He goes up town as soon after supper as he can get ready and seldom gets home before 9.30 and sometimes later so it leaves me alone evenings. Of course it's foolish of me to feel so about it because the evenings are all the time he has and he must attend to some things.

++++ *Sun. May 19. Wednesday Bert worked as usual—and Thursday morning when the alarm went off at 5 and I started to get up Bert grabbed me and said, "Don't put me up any lunch today. I'm going to Big Creek."*

The next day Lora noted, "...today he worked for Van Deusen at building a house." There followed for Bert a series of small jobs until he could make the right contact.

WE HAVE A LITTLE LOG CABIN, PLASTERED UP AGAINST THE SIDE OF A MOUNTAIN

IN MAY OF 1901, Lora went for a week's stay with Clella and George Brown (*him* of Lora's early infatuation) living some miles east of Encampment; Clella and George were homesteading on Big Creek.

Big Creek, ++Thu. May 30. Well. I am at George Brown's now. Bert had been intending to let me come up yesterday with Leo Davis but Tuesday when he came home for dinner he said, "George will be down for dinner." and then went on to say that Clella had come as far as Indian Creek and I could take Nibs and go over with them. Of course I wanted to and I did. Rode in the buggy with George as far as Indian Creek & led Nibs and then rode Nib as far as Collins. When we got there it was so late (and the wind was blowing too) that we went up to the next ranch where Frank Bridges lives, (He is the man that took up Lyman's old place but he's running Collins' upper place now.) Mrs. Bridges (or Grace as I am going to call her) is very nice. Clella and I stayed there all night and George took Nibs and went on over, he had to on account of the chickens. The next morning Clella and I took the team and drove the rest of the way over. Poor George has been having the tooth-ache. He has an incubator and some brooders and is raising chickens and ducks.

+Sat. June 1. Yesterday I came around and was sick in bed all day. My "tummy" didn't ache but my back "O My". Clella was awfully good to me and doctored me up in great shape. Day before yesterday I wrote to Bert and [Mamma] and I rode over to the mailbox and mailed it.

Sun. June 2. We didn't do much of anything only monkey around and take care of the ducks and chickens.

Mon. June 3. We didn't do anything in particular. This morning I took a photo of the little ducks....I miss Bert so much....As Edna Wilcox says, "It is nice to be some body's darling." I am having a good time though.

Tue. June 4. George went over to Big Creek last night and didn't get home until late. He came by the mail-box and got two letters for me from Bert. But I was asleep when he came home so I didn't get them until this morning. He enclosed a letter from Mother for me. He had opened and read it. It has rained nearly every day since I have been gone and he didn't start for the Ferris–Haggarty with Frank until Saturday.

3.25 P.M. This morning I wrote to Bert and Mother and took the letters over to the mail-box. It has rained most of the time since I have been up here and it is dreadfully cold—"colder than Billy be damned," to quote George. It keeps Clella busy looking after the little chickens and ducks. O dear I want to see Bert. What am I going to do about it? I guess I'll just have to grin and bear it....

Photographer unknown
Lora with Kodak, June 1900

7.45 P.M. It snowed this afternoon. Clella and I got to cutting up and said some shocking things.

+*Tue. June 6. Yesterday afternoon George started out for Encampment He went horseback and Clella and I went with him as far as the Big Creek field He intended to come back today and if Bert is in town perhaps he will come up with George. Oh I hope he does. It seems to me I'd give most anything just to crawl into his arms and have him hold me there a while. That is the place I like best on earth to be. I took two photos of Clella this morning. 5.30 P.M. Oh, I've had just the loveliest time this afternoon. Just after dinner Clella sent me to the mail-box with a letter and I told her to look for me back when she saw me coming and went on up the road toward Pearl. I knew I wouldn't have time to go all the way but I wanted to go, anyway. I went clear to where we camped on Big Creek next to the last night out when we came from Colorado four years ago. Got back about 4.15 and picked some flowers on my way home. Enjoyed myself immensely Now if Bert would just come tonight I'd have had a really happy day. It's just lovely up there and I was so happy all the while I was up there.*

Sat. June 8. ...Frank and Grace are to come up tonight, and tomorrow if it is nice we are all going over to the Platt, fishing. Clella and I are going to see if we can talk George into letting us girls go horseback. He has a horse that I can ride and I could let one of the girls have Nibs because he is so gentle. Bert, if he comes at all, may not get here until late but we will have to leave Jim (the hired man) here anyway on account of the chickens. and if he gets here in time he can come on over where we are....

Sun. June 9. 8.20 A.M. Grace and Frank came last night and her little sister Francis, who is staying with her. We are getting ready to go fishing now.

Glen Cottage, Mon. June 10. 5.10 P.M. We all went fishing as we expected, only we girls didn't go horseback because George said Dolly wasn't safe for a woman. It wasn't to the Platt we went at all, only Clella thought it was to be. Frank and George had to see about a projected ditch, out of Big Creek and thought they would take us along and fish a little. We caught grass-hoppers for them and tried to fish a little ourselves and then loafed around camp until they came for dinner. They had caught one trout and we ate him for dinner. They fished some in the afternoon and caught three or four. Bert didn't come. Today George was coming down so I came along to save trouble. More tomorrow.

Tue. June 11. Well, I will "resoom and continue on"—backward. George and I got started from over there pretty reasonably early after a few tears on the part of Grace and Clella (Alas! their old men were going). Frank went as far as Collins with his buggy and carried my satchel and Kodak that far.

In addition to her more lengthy trips, Lora was quick to "pay a visit to" or "be paid a visit by" her young town acquaintances or the cousins, especially Carrie ("Tad") and Maggie ("Daisy"). As usual, Bert's frequent business jaunts to the hills sent her quickly down to Mum's. Willow Glen, as it had been before the marriages of the girls, continued to be a gathering place; some essence of the pre–Grand Encampment days survived. Lora's return there seemed to signify a return to the old life, a life not always pleasing to Bert.

Aunt Nan and Carrie, at home

*Tue. July 9, 1901. This morning Charley started out
to the railroad to be gone three days and Lib came
down here. We ironed. Tad and Maggie came, just as
we were eating dinner and in the afternoon, we
danced and then fixed up a "teeter" (alias see-saw) in
the grove. Teetered on that for a while and Lib made
some taffy which was very good. About four Maggie
went home and this evening Tad and I teetered and
I read more of "Sentimental Tommy." We go to discussing how nice it would be if I were only her boy
cousin and she has decided to call me "Dick." Bert
has not come yet. He may come tomorrow. I am having such a nice time, I almost wish he wouldn't come
but I miss him dreadfully whenever I stop "Howling
around" long enough to think....Our teeter is lots of
fun. We had a "holy picnic" putting up cross pieces
on two trees for it to rest on.*

Wush't I Wuz A Boy

(Lisa Ann's Lament!)

Wush't I wuz a boy!
So's I could jump and run
And yell real loud, and whistle
An' fite, an have the mostest fun
Like boys duz
Wush't I wuz a boy!

Wush't I wuz a boy!
So's maw won't allus say:
"Don't straddle the fence now, Liza Ann
Nice girls don't do that way."
But boys duz—
Wush't I wuz a boy!

Wush't I wuz a boy!
'N when they call me names,
"Tom-boy," "tag-tail," an' "whistlin Ann"
'N I could fite same's
Billy duz
Wush't I wuz a boy!

Wush't I wuz a boy!
'N me an' John could play
At "skin the cat" an' leap frog too
My dress is in the way—
Boys' pants ain't
Wush't I wuz a boy!

Wush't I wuz a boy!
All girls' good fur—jist
To dust an' sweep an' schold [*sic*]
An' sew on buttons what yo' mis't
Sewin' on last week.
Wush't I wuz a boy!

Wush't I wuz a boy!
Wush't God'd made gurls boys,
An' made boys gurls—'ud been the same,
'N I'd bin John an' John bin
Liza Ann by name,
Wush't he had
Wush't I wuz a boy!

(+Sat. Dec. 7. [1901])

*Wed. July 10. Today, Pop went fishing with Mr.
Andrews and a gang and so he let Tad and I have
Colonel to ride. We went down to Lebou's after my
side-comb I lost at the dance and got there at dinner
time....We started from Lebou's about 2.20 and
stopped at Maggie's for a while. I put on a suit of
Dave's clothes (with a sofa cushion stuffed in the
front to fill out the "tum-tum") and nearly convulsed
them with laughter. We came on up home and just
before we got to Encampment we met Frank and
Grace Bridges. They were eating candy and gave us
some. They had seen Bert in town so of course I was
in a thundering hurry....*

*Tue. July 16. Whoop! This afternoon as Tad and I
were reposing under the trees here came Len and
Emery and they came over where we were and they
had come up to tell us Shafes are going to have a little dance tomorrow night. Now I want to go—awfully but Bert doesn't like to go to that kind of dance
and he doesn't like me to go when he isn't here and I
do want to do as he wishes but it's so hard, when
they are all going and I would have to answer so
many questions. I'm a coward. 9 P.M. This evening
after supper Tad and I went to town for some things.
It was cool and nice and we enjoyed the walk down.
We got to ride back with Gene and Nora. They just
got back from Pearl. Tad and I picked strawberries*

*this morning and had short-cake for dinner. Pop
went to Beaver Creek.*

*+Thu. July 18, [1901] . Yesterday we monkeyed
around and didn't get much done. Bert got back
from the Ferris–Haggarty where he went the day
before after his possessions. We went to the dance.
Tad, Bert and I rode down with Dell, Nora, Ola,
Ethel Ladd and the baby. And Oh Lord! They have a
little bite of a house with two rooms in it and old
Lebou played most of the time—and you know what
that means. Well—I got into all sorts of trouble. Bert
was tired and disgusted and cross as two sticks and
I rowed around awfully I suppose, tho I didn't know
it. Toward morning one time Tad and I got up and
two-stepped to a tune Lebou was playing and then
Jen and Mayme got up and we ran them down and
then after a short rest, Mayme and Kid Bryan got up
and we ran them down and pretty soon Bert came
out there as mad as a wet hen and stopped us. Well I
was mad for a minute awfully mad. As Cliff used to
say, "I'd ha' fit a buzz saw." I hadn't thought how it
would look. We came home pretty soon then and
there was thunder in the atmosphere. Carrie, Ola
and I were riding in the back seat and Bert was
standing up behind us. He had his hand on my
shoulder to steady himself and pretty soon he put
his hand under my chin and tipped my head back so
we looked into each other's eyes. That won the day. I
was still feeling rather sore—of course about nothing
but after that I was sorry. We came on home and
went to bed.*

*I woke up about 8.30 and heard the gang getting
ready to go fishing so I got up. Pop, Mum, Lib and
Charley went, and Bert, Carrie and I stayed to run
things. We had just finished breakfast when here
they came back. Pop had got a "call." After Carrie
and I got the dishes done we went out to teeter.*

Pretty soon Bert came out and said he wanted to talk to me, so I went and we leaned on the fence— and talked. yes indeed! We did talk. And he said if I didn't care for him any more he would go away and he said I had snubbed him and glared at him and several things of a like nature and come to find out it was all about Len and my talking and dancing with him so much. And he said it was a mistake us getting married and that I ought to have married a young fellow who would have gone and taken his pleasure and let me take mine. But I agree with that woman of historic fame who says, "Better be an old man's darling than a young man's slave." Besides I don't think Bert is too old. You know he is only ten years older than I, really. And I am an Oldman's darling. After he had said all he had to say he went to town and I stumbled over into the grove, threw myself on the grass and cried a little while and then I sat there and looked out at the road.

Pop was hitching up his horse and pretty soon he came over and said," What's the matter?"

"Nothing."

"What are you doing?"

"Just rubbering."

"What are you rubbering at?"

"Nothing—just rubbering."

Then he got down on his knees and peeped into my face. Then he gathered me into his arms and said, "Don't tell Papa there's nothing the matter. I know there is." I cried some more then and he said," You've got one friend left, baby." Pretty soon he asked me if I could tell him and I did tell him a little about Len and he said," Don't cry about it. It isn't worth it. If he is going to be so unreasonable I suppose he will." Then he asked if this was the first time Bert had flared up and I said yes. He didn't say anything then for quite a while and then he said," I can't say much about this but you've always got a place to go.

You don't have to stand this one minute more than
you want to." I looked at him then and his eyes were
full of tears. He laughed then and said, "I tell you
not to cry and then go right ahead and do it myself."
He whipped out his handkerchief, changed the sub-
ject and that is the last that has been said.

++Tue. July 23. Sunday morning the gang got ready
to go fishing and Bert said I might go so I flew
around and got ready and went—like a green fool—
and I know he didn't want me to go. He didn't kiss
me Good-Bye and he looked so sorry and forsaken.
Before we were half way over, I regretted having
gone. Tad & Maggie rode horseback and Pop,
Charley, Mamma, Aunt Nan, Lizzie and I all rode in
the wagon and about half way over I "spelled"
Carrie. We got over there, got ourselves some dinner
and the men hiked out a fishing and about four
o'clock, Maggie and Carrie, Lib and I went swim-
ming. The men got back just in time to pitch the tent
before dark. Monday Mum, Aunt Nan and I went
gooseberrying and when we got back, Aunt Nan,
Maggie, Lib and I went in swimming. We went again
after dinner only Lib didn't. It was all something
like the old life. The camp coffee and stars especially.
At night I stuck my head out from under the tent
and looked at the stars & it was nice but oh, it
would have been so much nicer to have my darling
Bert's arms around me and feel his heart beating
against my own....

Eventually, Mr. Bohrer wanted Bert to help "prove
up" on the claims on Miner Creek. At the same time
Lora exalted over her return to Cosy Cottage; she and
Bert had been renting two rooms from Mike Whalen
while the Bentleys occupied the cottage. In August,

Lora made the happy discovery of the Van Deusen
cabin, where she could join Bert while he worked.

*Cosy Cottage, Fri. July 26, 1901. We moved down to
our own little home today. It seems so nice to be here
again. Our darling little home! The front room is
papered and looks very nice. We straightened the
kitchen and back bed-room today and Bert is going
to paint the wood-work in the front rooms and paper
the bed-room with the same kind of paper as the sitting room before we straighten around any....This
evening while Bert was gone, Mr. Bohrer, the blind
man who lets Bert run some of his property, came
over with a friend to see Bert. He wouldn't wait
because he was tired and told me to tell Bert he was
here and have him come to see him, Mr. B., tomorrow. Bert got home a few minutes after Mr. Bohrer
left and started out after him immediately.*

*++Sat. Aug. 10. Thursday I ironed and Friday I
intended to scrub but Bert gave me a whole day off
so I went to Mamma's. He went with me and stayed
to dinner. Then he came on down town and stayed
until about five and then came home with a whole
market-basket full of my possessions. Friday evening
the expected letter and check from Mr. Bohrer came,
to begin work on the Colorado Belle. We intend to go
Monday so Bert has been busy hunting out camp
outfits, making a grub list, etc. ....*

*Van Deusen Cabin, Tuesday. Aug. 13. ...This morn-
ing I got started for here about 9.15 and got here,
sound of wind and limb, at about 10.20. You remember, a long time ago, Bert took a picture of the interi-
or of this cabin when the Van Deusen boys were living here. It is a very good picture. I didn't think then
that I would ever be living in it though. Oh, it's just
simply lovely here. There are lots of trees and the*

creek runs right by the cabin. I turned Nibs loose and managed to keep him here until about six o-clock and then he got away and went home. Bert is going down tomorrow and says he will bring him up. I like it here, awfully. It's nicer than anything I've struck since I can remember.

Wed. Aug. 14. Today Bert went to town after some things. He got such a late start he didn't get back for dinner, so Mr. Doyle ate dinner in solitary state. Now I'm going to say something awful. You know Bert is so particular about letting me do some things, like going to Saratoga alone, and it's on a main traveled road too—and he can let me be up here all alone with Mr. Doyle—forty miles from no-where. There that's all. This evening, I went up the trail toward the tunnel, to within a little ways of it. Bert didn't bring Nibs—but I can go and get him.

Thu. Aug. 15. The men took their lunch today, and I rounded up all the dirty flour sacks etc. and washed them—prowled around and straightened the cabin a little. It is a lovely place here and I like it. Tomorrow if nothing happens to prevent, I am going down to the ranch, and get Nibbs. I have to go to town too. As I want a picket rope and some shoes. Just before I came up I sent for some film for the Kodak so pretty soon I can take some more pictures. The trail coming in here is a hummer. It is an impossibility to come clear in with a wagon and things have to be packed about 3/4 of a mile or more on burros. The trail up to the tunnel is simply awful—that is it would seem so to any one not used to mountain trails. Lots of the Van Dusen Boys' things are here—among others a whole shelf of books—I won't do a thing—have read one and part of another. It is convenient their being kind enough to let Bert have their cabin.

Van Duesen Cabin

Fri. Aug. 16. 7.45 P.M. This morning I hurried up and got my work done and then hit the pike for Grand Encampment. It was about 8.30 when I started. Duke went with me I took about an hour to go to the ranch. Stopped there a little while saddled up Nibbs and went on to town to do my errands. Got a real good pair of shoes and a picket rope. Stayed at Mum's for dinner and about three, saddled up Nibbs and came home. I picketed him by the cabin tonight. That is pretty close and tomorrow I am going to take him up the canyon where there is good feed. Tomorrow evening Bert intends to go to town and he is going to take me and come back Sunday. This dear delightful spot! Oh, I love it already.

+Mon. Aug. 19. Yesterday Aunt Nan and Mamma went up to Lizzie's to dinner. I couldn't go, because

Grub Shelf in the Van Duesen Cabin

Bert had gone to town after a burro, intending to go up and pack some timbers to the tunnel and I didn't know when he would come along. I read and mon-keyed-around until one-o-clock and then he came along....Bert took his burro and went on up the hill....Bert got down out of the hills in time for sup-per but was so tired that he decided we'd stay there overnight so we did. He came up this forenoon and I pieced quilt blocks until dinner and then went to town & got some things, came back and picked up my leavings and hit the pike for camp and here I was is. Bert, the rascal has been reading my diary. Well if he ever gets this far he will find out that he is a scamp. O <u>Wow</u>!

The mining companies were having trouble with the lumber shortage; it was not only almost impossible to

The Van Duesen's Doorway

get the lumber in the first place, but there was still the problem of getting it transported to the claims where they wanted to erect their shaft houses and other buildings. The lowly burro played a very important part in the development of the camp; these sure-footed little beasts could go practically anywhere a man could walk, and all sorts of needed supplies were thus packed into the claims that were being developed. Mr. H E Ball utilized 2 burros, one ahead of the other, tandem style, to pack in some lumber, 12 or 14 foot boards strapped on each side of the burros; he said he did not have any trouble only in "rounding the corners" on trails that were far from straight. It was really quite an achievement. One of the funniest sights I ever saw was a wheel-barrow being packed in for the Colorado Belle group of claims on Miner Creek. It had been strapped, right side up, right on the top of the pack-saddle; this was a very small burro, "The Blue Jinny" in case any of you remember her, and the wheel-barrow reached to her tail and well up on her neck; my husband, Bert Oldman, was leading her and I was walking down the trail behind her. They went through a steep little gully, and as they reached the bottom and started up, ALL I could see was a moving wheelbarrow with a tail switching at one end and donkey ears wagging at the other. The little beast was entirely obscured.

(IR 65)

Lora divided her time between camp at the Van Duesen cabin and trips afoot or on Nibs to Cosy Cottage at Grand Encampment, Willow Glen, or Lizzie's ranch. She was especially occupied with the Kodak and her experiments in developing.

+*Mon. Aug. 26. Printed some pictures and speaking of pictures I sent for some "Velox" Paper. It prints black and white and can be printed by lamp-light I also sent for some more blue print paper.*

Thu. Aug. 29. Today I baked bread and pies etc. and took some pictures. One of the canyon above the cabin. One of Duke sitting in the trail, one of the cabin and another of the cabin the way it looks from the trail, which was a failure. The rest are good.

Tue. Sept. 3. I stayed at the ranch all day while Bert went to Miner and back. Tried my Velox paper and failed most dismally. However I shall try again and keep at it until I succeed.

When the work on the Colorado Belle claims was completed in October, Bert rambled the District and picked up what work he wanted.

*Sat. Oct. 12. Bert says he is going up to the
Kurtz–Chatterton Country to do some work on a
claim...*

*++++Tue. Oct. 22. This morning he started out with
a surveying party who are going to survey a railroad line from here to Walcott.*

*+Wed. Oct. 30. Bert went to work at the smelter
today....This evening I got letters from Clella and
Carrie and Bert got one from Mr. Bohrer, containing
a check for $100. Bert thinks of going on a survey
with Mr. Countryman soon.*

But then Mr. Bohrer engaged Bert for another job at
the Home Fraction claims and also offered Lora a job in
camp. Then, Mr. Bohrer mentioned a possibility which
made Lora speculate.

*Thu. Oct. 31. Bert did go surveying today—up in the
Ferris–Haggarty country. He is to be gone about a
week. I am staying at the ranch while he is gone. Mr.
Bohrer sent the money to do the work on the "Sugar
Loaf"—that is over in the Charter Oak country, and
he suggested having Bert come to Colorado when he
gets this work done and look to his (Mr. B.'s) property there. Jehu! Wouldn't that be a fright? What
would I do if I had to leave here? How could I ever
get along without Mamma? And I would have to sell
Nibs!*

*Home Fraction, Fri. Nov. 15. 7.45 P.M. Bert came to
the ranch Thursday evening and today I came over
with him. Say boys! This is the prettiest place you
ever saw. I'm in love with it already. We have a little
log cabin, plastered up against the side of a mountain and we have the finest view imaginable of the
surrounding country. This is just fine. The lamp,*

*(elevated upon an inverted basin), is lighted, and
there are dim shadows in the corners of the room.
Bert is sitting by the table reading a newspaper.
There is a pair of elk horns in one of the gables. Our
three weeks "grub" supply is stored in some corner
shelves. The meat-chopper, clock and an empty cigar-
box, hob-nob on a shelf.*

*Sat. Nov. 16. I explored around a little bit, today.
Bert showed me the other cabins, where Miss Moore
was when she worked out here. They are just along
the road a little farther from our cabin, and past
them is the shaft house where we keep Nibs. The
men come here to eat but they always "hike out" as
soon as they are through....This is a soft snap. I like
it. And then you know I will have some dollars when
I get through....*

*Sat. Nov. 23. Bert had Jack Smith take the saddle-
horse back today. Mr. Smith is coming back tomorrow and then he is going to let Bert have the team to
go after some hay for Nibs. Nibbie don't much like
being alone and every time I go out he whinnies so
cute at me. I took him to water today. There is going
to be a big dance at Encampment, Thanksgiving
night but I don't know whether we will go or not.
This cabin is way up on the side of a mountain,
nearly to the top, and we have a lovely view of the
surrounding country. We can see the Encampment
River, from the Baggott rocks, up nearly to Riverside
and Cow Creek, Calf Creek and Spring Creek. We
can see Saratoga and by climbing a little ways up to
the top of the mountain we can see Encampment.
The wind blows all of the time, and everything that
is left loose goes rolling merrily down the mountain
side. The cabin faces downhill of course and the
road goes along in front. We had an empty barrel sitting out by the end of the cabin and last evening,*

when a particularly hard gust of wind came along,
it went bounding down the mountain and once it
jumped about 20 ft in the air It never stopped till it
got to the bottom and landed up against a pine, with
one of its staves knocked in and the hoops all loose.

It was during this stay with Bert at Mr. Bohrer's Home Fraction that Lora had an adventure with one of the mining district's most famous (or, perhaps, infamous) characters, Alkali Ike. Lora quoted the *Herald*'s characterization of Ike as it appeared in a premature obituary, and Ike's own retraction of the obituary along with her personal account.

ALKALI IKE IS DEAD

Alkali Ike is dead. World renowned as he was through the medium of Bill Nye's pen as a typical western character, he was none the less so for having been written in a story. Alkali Ike was the real thing without exaggeration. He was fated. He died with his boots on.

Ike left no autobiography by which a synopsis of his life could be obtained but he has been known to talk occasionally about himself when in the mood and he has told some great tales on himself.

There are several versions of the origin of his nickname, but it is sufficient that Bill Nye had good reason for naming him Alkali, which might have been intended as an inflection of alcohol.

With all his varied experience, Ike has been principally engaged, during the closing years of his illustrious life, in the cause of temperance, having taken on a personal responsibility in putting down liquor.

"Calamity Ike" would have been as appropriate for Daniel Bellews as Alkali. Ike was always having an accident. It was a black eye, or a wounded foot, or a broken jaw, or something, anything; and it was all the time. Reports from Fort Steele, where he expired, state that Ike broke his jaw again and quit the earth.

Alkali Ike has gone over the range to his reward. The memory of this odd character will fade with the frontier history of Wyoming.

ALKALI IKE NOT A DEAD ONE
Says He Will Outlive The Lobster Who Started The Report

Fort Steele, Wyo., June 1—(special)—"Alkali Ike" respectfully declines to accept the report as true that he is dead. He says it is a —— lie and that he will outlive the ?!?!?! —— who started the report. ....

(GEH/IR. 293–4)

Ike was around Encampment most of the time, during the earliest days of the camp: he was a hard rock miner of no mean ability and also a good teamster, and could always get work whenever he really wanted a job. After weeks, or maybe months, of trying to "drink the town dry," he would go out on some job far from town and there he would stay, doing good and faithful work for his employer until the unquenchable thirst finally drew him back to town to complete the cycle once more.

(IR, 294)

One day when I had been walking around the Home Fraction cabins taking pictures, I saw a team and wagon approaching the Foyle camp; however, they did not stop there, but started the climb to our camp. Mr. Oldman had not spoken about ordering any supplies so I had no idea what was the occasion for these visitors. It was a long slow climb up that mountain, and with a load took an hour or more. I went back to our cabin and started a fire, on the possible chance it might be someone who could stay to dinner.

No time was wasted in road making, around these camps, just bare essentials. On this step hillside, a space but little wider than the wagon itself had been leveled for travel, in front of our cabin, the hill falling away steeply beyond it; in order to turn around, it was necessary to drive on to the Home Fraction nearby, where a meager space for turning had been cleared. A wide turn of the climb up the mountain took the team out of sight for a little way before the final turn brought it right in front of the cabin—practically on the doorstep in fact.

As it swung into sight again, my heart dropped into my boots; there was nobody in that wagon but Alkali Ike slumped forward with his hat over his eyes, and the hand holding the reins dangling between his knees. For no reason I had always feared Alkali Ike, probably because I had never seen him otherwise than bleary-eyed and weaving with drink. I think if there had been a knot-hole in the back of that cabin, I would have crawled through it!

No escape! The only window was beside the door, and the wagon was just drawing up in front of them. So, as I knew there was nothing else to do, I marched across that cabin with my chin up, as my mother would have done and threw open the door. Ike had stopped the team, and as I threw open the door, the red-rimmed eyes under the lowered hat-brim gave a long level look at that seventeen year old girl standing in the door; then he straightened up, raised his hat and said, "Where do you want this grub, ma'am?"

I said, "Just set the boxes in on the table please. I can put things on the shelves." So that is what he did. Then he drove on to the turn-around and soon came past the cabin on his way down the hill, raising his hat again as he passed.

(IR, 296–7)

Lora anticipated her paycheck; "I am getting paid a dollar a day for cooking over here. Bert started my time from when he came over, so I have fifteen dollars coming now" (Sun. Nov. 24). However, when she went to the ranch to celebrate Thanksgiving of 1901, a septic throat, an old enemy, altered her plans.

> *Tue. Nov. 26. Oh, I do wish I hadn't got this blamed*
> *sore throat..."how sum ever," my health is worth*
> *more than the dollars and I might have been laid up*
> *all winter. I am such a "no count" thing any way.*

She remained at Cosy Cottage or, more often, at the ranch with Mamma while Bert completed the work at the Home Fraction and went on to travel the district for Mr. Bohrer throughout the winter of 1901–1902. The hills were never closed; travelers were only temporarily detained.

> *Friday Dec. 13. It has been bitterly cold all day. This*
> *afternoon, I took Duke out for a run and nearly froze*
> *my poor little nose. Bert doesn't think he can get*
> *away tomorrow but will wait and go Sunday. I am*
> *afraid he will just freeze up there. It is so cold.*

THREE FAT WHITE SPECIMENS
OF THE PORCINE SPECIES

WHILE LORA LAMENTED Bert's absences and celebrated his frequent visits, she had a jolly seventeenth winter, that last winter of her adolescence. Her diary entries were as full of exuberance as her days. It began with the family Thanksgiving:

> *Wed. Nov. 27. We dream turkey, talk pumpkin pie, and think cranberries.*

> *++Sat. Nov. 30. Uncle Ez's folks were up and we ate turkey till we nearly sprouted feathers and had a nice time.*

It continued through Christmas, even though Bert was marooned in the hills. "I nearly forgot to mention that Lizzie made for me a cover, for the lid of my *Po* and put on it 'Peace be still!' Wouldn't that curl your whiskers?—so to speak. (Merry Christmas)."

Many of her thoughts focused on the Kodak. With Bert working steadily and with her few dollars earned cooking for the miners, economy wasn't foremost.

> *Sun. Dec. 1. 1901. ...When I took the Kodak over to the Home Fraction, I wanted to get a picture of the*

Baby Herring, held in the pathway

Charter Oak as I came by but it was snowing Billy Guns and I couldn't. I want to see if I can get any sort of a picture of the smelter. There is a good place here in this house, I think, to take "portraits" and I am going to take one of Mamma and if they are any good I will have her take one of me. When Lizzie sent her freight order, I sent for a lot of photographic materials so when they get here I will have enough to last me a little while. In that order, I included a new ruby lamp as mine was somewhat combusticated. Daisy, (more properly Maggie) sent for a couple of green glass trays for me a Christmas present.

Sisters Bessie and Edith Kennady, with ducks

They are very nice. I believe I have got more fun out of that camera, than anything else I ever owned, unless it was the guitar. Oh—I don't know though—there is the pony and lots of things....

Sat. Jan. 11, 1902. Lindy, Gene, & Annie F. were up today to have the children's pictures. I took two of Henry and Clarence and two of Annie's baby and then to finish up the roll of film, I took one of Tad.

Sunday, Jan. 12. I tried to develope that film last night and my "dad-bing-de-jewed" new ruby lamp light-struck it.

In January Lora went to Toga twice and gave the camera good exercise there in documenting Mrs. Cluff's house, three pigs roaming the streets, and the then considered humorous spectacle of three females,

Kennady Sisters
In a buggy, with Margarette and Mrs. Andrews

On the Burro
Mrs. Lewis is holding Edgar Vane; Dewey Dunlap is in the saddle;
Goldie Anderson holds her baby as Mayme Dunlap stands by.

Photographer unknown
Henry Herring, creeping
Lora, Annie Hickok, and Gary Herring are in the background.

considered humorous spectacle of three females, including herself, taking turns dressing in male attire.

Thursday, Jan. 23. ...Yesterday I took the camera over to Mrs. Cluff's and took some pictures for her; of her flowers and the dining room and the front of the house. Then I saw three fat white specimens of the porcine species out in the road and sallied forth to photograph them. I followed them around for quite a

Cluff House in Saratoga

while, much to the amusement of the stage driver,
"anoder" man and several small boys....

+Sunday, Feb. 2. ...Yesterday Tad and I went over to
Tot's and Tad dressed up in Clark's clothes & I took
two pictures of her & Tot, then I "wore the pants"
and was "took" with Tad and then with Tot. This
morning I took another interior of Aunt Nan's house.

This particular winter brought Lizzie and Lora
together often as Charley was freighting and Bert gone
to the hills. Lora had a new musical interest:

Dec. 2, Monday. I am learning to play the guitar by
the American method and getting along famously.
When Lizzie was here...she played the fiddle and I
played seconds for her so I got lots of practice.

Mrs. Cluff's Dining Room

Lora dutifully copied in Diary the new songs she and Lizzie learned. On December 5th, "This is a song and I think it is cute. Its the 'Song That Shocked Chicago,' so it must be."

Everybody Wondered How He Knew

There are often little trifles which are better left unsaid
But are uttered in an unaffected way,
Which reminds me of a funny little matter which occurred
At a fashionable ball the other day.
The host espied a silk embroidered garter on the floor,
And gaily dared the owner to declare,

When a jolly looking fellow said without the least
  concern,
"Oh, I know, it belongs to Mrs. Dare."

Now wasn't that a silly thing to say?
Wasn't it a silly thing to do?
It came as quite a starter
When he recognized that garter
For everybody wondered how he knew.
Now wasn't that a silly thing to say?
Wasn't it a silly thing to do?
But they didn't hear 'til later
That she'd got them from his mater
So everybody wondered how he knew.

They were crowding round the baby at a christening
After which he was handed round for everyone to
  see;
And a circumstance which somehow
Seemed to please the people most
Was a dainty little dimple on his knee.
Said Cousin Jack from Oxford who was staying
  there just then
"This looks like a hereditary strain.
For isn't it a funny thing
That just in this respect,
He's exactly like his elder sister Jane."

Now wasn't that a silly thing to say?
Wasn't it a silly thing to do?
It was really worse than simple
When he talked about that dimple
For everybody wondered how he knew.
Wasn't that a silly thing to say?
Wasn't it a silly thing to do?
Yet he chanced to see that dimple
While out bathing—ain't that simple?
But everybody wondered how he knew.

Folks were gazing at the very latest painting at a
    sale
Labeled "Beauty Unadorned" upon the list
When a gentleman remarked to several others
    standing by
"It's not true—such perfect beauty can't exist."
"Excuse me, sir," a gentleman remarked, "but you
    are wrong.
And if you like I'll bet this case of fizz
That this painting here before you is exactly true to
    life
And represents the girl just as she is."

Now wasn't that a silly thing to say?
Wasn't it a silly thing to do?
The ladies blushed and wiggled
And the men turned round and giggled
For everybody wondered how he knew.
Wasn't that a silly thing to say?
Wasn't it a silly thing to do?
Yet nothing could be quainter
You see, he was the painter.
Yet everybody wondered how he knew.

They were eagerly discussing different reasons for
    divorce
At a dinner when a married man opined
That snoring loud on either side should constitute a
    case,
For it sufficed to drive you off your mind
"Quite right," remarked a smartly dressed young
    lady to a friend,
"I never snore. By any chance, do you?"
On hearing which her fiancee absent-mindedly
    remarked,
"Don't tell such stories, dear, you know you do."

Now wasn't that a silly thing to say?
Wasn't it a silly thing to do?
It not only sounded shady
But it quite upset the lady
For everybody wondered how he knew.
Wasn't that a silly thing to say?
Wasn't it a silly thing to do?
Until he said, "Don't scold me.
Your sister Fannie told me."
Why everybody wondered how he knew.

The visual appearance of Lora's diary was altered frequently during this winter. She assigned numbers to the letters of the alphabet and wrote several entire entries and parts of others in the resulting code. Lora was entertaining herself as well as playing a joke on anyone who ventured to read the diary and decipher the code. The selections were wildly romantic, purple prose involving a "Mr. Gordon" and a mountain reverie.

> *Friday, Jan. 3, 1902. ...Mysterious shadows of the gathering night across a gorge came faint and with sad sweetness the cry of some wandering night bird, then the wind caught up the cry and carried it away in the silent darkness of the night and a great longing came to me and my heart....*

There appears the "form of a woman" with "breath of the jasmine garden" and "hair which hid her face like a cloak of gold." She ends the entry with "Wouldn't that jar you!"

By February, 1901, Bert and Lora were once more at Cosy Cottage most of the time. Bert was helping Frank Cramer survey the line for the coming tramway which was to connect the Ferris–Haggarty to the new smelter. Lora was so enjoying the companionship of her town friends, especially the Wilcox girls, Edna (Teddie) and Belle, who were soon to be brides, that an important decision by Bert rated only an aside in her diary entry of Monday, Feb. 24, 1902.

> *Saturday I loafed over at Wilcox's most all day. In the evening we went to the dance. The crowd just fit the hall and everyone seemed to have a good time. Yesterday we slept pretty late and in the afternoon we went up to the ranch. And do you know Bert is thinking of renting the ranch and he and Papa talked as though they might come to an agreement. Eva sent me a nice book of guitar music. I was so pleased to get it. At the dance Mr. Myers said he would like to borrow my old guitar book because it has the Faust Marches in it and he never before saw them arranged for the guitar. Teddie and Belle were over this afternoon. Tomorrow is Libsey's birthday, her twentieth birthday. She and I used to think that when we got to be respectively, sixteen and eighteen we would just be somebody and here we are, eighteen and twenty.*

Bert did rent the ranch from Lora's Pop. Since Horace and Sylvia now occupied their new two-story log house, the homestead cabin, "Glen Cottage," was available for Bert and Lora. The ranch was, in essence, a family affair. The two girls, although both had their own homes, never had distanced themselves from Mamma. Charley never had abandoned the role of hired hand and he and Horace shared horses, pasture, equipment, and chores with no formalities. Bert, Lora's husband of almost two years and frequent visitor to Willow Glen, remained a visitor, someone from the outside.

For reasons Lora never expressed, a dissension, a rivalry had grown between Bert and Charley.

> *Sun. May 19, 1901. Bert intended to help Pop on the fence tomorrow but Chas. is to help and Bert says he can't work with Chas.*

According to Lora, Bert's antagonism toward Charley grew intense.

> *Sat. July 13, 1901. You know Bert and Charley hate each other cordially and today Bert told me if I had any regard for his wishes I would never go inside their house again. Wouldn't that jar you?*

> *Mon. Dec. 9, 1901. It is such a horrid nuisance having Sir Charles, the knight of the Rueful Countenance, in the family. We can't have any "family reunion" this Christmas, "at all, at all." I am quite lost at the prospect of not taking Christmas dinner at the ranch.*

Lora did spend Christmas, as usual, at Mamma's and reported on that day, "We had a very nice time." Bert was snowbound in the hills.

As Bert generally acted autonomously, he may not have shared with Lora his rationale for renting the ranch. There was but one obvious consideration for the move. Apparently, Bert's lease from Horace did not include absolute control of the entire property and all its activities. In addition, Bert continued to maintain his mining interests. However, movements went apace after Horace agreed to the rental, and Bert was soon on his way to becoming his perception of a farmer.

Early in April, the chores of the move paused while the young Oldmans, with Mamma, attended the social event of Grand Encampment's spring. American popular entertainment at the turn of the century often relied upon the incongruities—and crudities—offered by blackface and the ethnic song or joke. Yet, the editor of the *Herald*, himself a composer and participant in the show, had only applause for this effort by the city's leading citizens. Lora commented on the singing.

> *Willow Glen, ++Wednesday, April 2. Monday, we moved some of our things up here and we stayed at Mum's all night—yesterday morning I had to go to town with Bert to sign a paper. We had to mortgage our house for $200.00 as we had to have some money. Last night the Home Talent minstrel show came off. Mamma, Bert and I went. It was really very good. They had some splendid singing....*

The home talent minstrel show, given for the benefit of the local fire department was far and away the event of the year in the line of social, musical and dramatic entertainment. The large audience was genuinely surprised at the excellence of the performance as an artistic whole, and at the individual brilliancy of the participants. Nothing but enthusiastic commendation of the entertainment has been heard from those who attended.

After a rousing opening chorus, Mr. Thad Kyner gave the first solo of the evening, the. coon song, "I Hates to Get Up Early in the Morn." Mr. Kyner has a rich mellow voice, and an unusual command of the darky [*sic*] dialect, which makes him a particularly competent interpreter of coon [*sic*] songs....

Fred Watt then got in the game with the uproarious coon [*sic*] song, "My Gal's Done Wrong." Watt's personal popularity insured him a hearty welcome, and his spirited singing and razor-play won him loud applause.

One of the most appreciated numbers was Carl Ashley's "Cunnin' Carolina Coon," his sweet boyish voice ringing out in the solo and leading the chorus with splendid effect.

George Kuntzman made a hit with his parody, "Far Far Away." His local allusions kept the audience in a roar, and he was recalled again and again till his lines were ausgerspielt!

The touching theme and tender melody of "The Tie That Binds" was splendidly rendered by W L Sill and his song was universally commended as one of the most pleasing features of the evening....

Throughout the first part the audience had been kept in good humor by the steady fire of jokes, gags, puns and stories from the end men...with the able assistance of the interlocutor H D Ashley.

The Hebrew sketch by Messrs Smizer and Kuntzman kept the audience in convulsions....

The grand finale was furnished by four prize-winners from Constantine, Michigan, whose names and whiskers served to disguise Messrs. Fred Watt, John Yensel, Clyde and Earle Clemens. These "Michigan Hay Huskers" sang a humorous travesty composed by Mr. Earle R Clemens, dealing with their various adventures in and about Grand Encampment which sent the audience home in a hilarious mood.

(GEH/IR 100–103)

Thursday, April 3. Straightened things up some more. This dear old wreck of a house—it is just going to pieces. It has stood here for sixteen years now and as it is an awfully wet place the logs are rotting out and letting it sink down. Here is a picture of it as it always looked when we all lived here. Bert and Dell have been hauling hay over from the field for the last two days....

Friday, April 4. Bert cleaned out the milk house and straightened up the yard some today. This forenoon Mamma and Lizzie were up to see me. This evening when I went down after the milk (Mamma gives us about a quart, cream and all, and all the skim milk we want). Mamma "halved up" on the flower seeds she had. I am going to try and raise some morning glories, pansies, sweet peas, nasturtiums, and mignonette.

Saturday, April 19. I feel somewhat better tonight, and have been since noon. Mamma was up this morning and stayed until after dinner, then I went down with her and stayed until time to come home and get supper. This evening Bert went to town and took me with him. It is a moon-lit night and nice and warm. I enjoyed the ride very much. Had a letter from Mother this evening.

Not long ago Bert sent for an incubator and a brooder and we are going to try and raise some poultry. And I completely forgot to mention our new cow. One day while I was in bed, Bert and Dell went over to Beaver Creek to look at a cow that was for sale. She looked pretty good so Bert bought her—paid $60 for her and a steer calf. She is a dear old thing and so gentle. Papa thinks Bert got quite a bargain. She gives her milk down nicely too.

++Wednesday. April 30. Sunday, we cut some potato-seed and Monday Bert planted one patch and I washed. We looked for Papa and Mamma home last night but they didn't come. Today I took a picture down by the water-hole. Yesterday I took one of Goldfinder. Yesterday Bert went over to Beaver Creek and bought 19 hens and two roosters.

Monday. May 5. Papa, Dell and Bert burned brush and we all ate at Mamma's. Our incubator brooder etc. came this evening.

+++Friday. May 9. Last night I stayed at Mum's & today Pop and Bert are planting spuds. For the past few days they have been burning brush and plowing Pop's garden. This afternoon I went to Mrs. Dettinger's & got four dozen eggs. We had got four dozen of Noah Wagoner before so we can set the incubator.

++++++++++Tuesday, May 20. On the eleventh we set the incubator. Lizzie was over to Mamma's to stay all night on the 15th and we both stayed there. Yesterday and the day before, it snowed and some today too. It is quite interesting running the incubator. On the 15th I tested the eggs and am going to again tonight. I guess I didn't tell you about our Belgian Hares at all. Bert got two bred does and a buck from Andrews and Dr. Perdue gave him a pair. We got a dear old cat and three kittens from Dettinger.

I TELL YOU IT WAS A SNAP

THEN, IN THE MIDST OF ALL THIS FECUNDITY, Lora dropped
her secret to Diary:

> +++++*Mon. May 26. The Redmen gave a dance last
> Thursday. We all attended. It was a hot dance. Two
> of our Belgians have little ones. I have just finished
> reading "Bob—Son of Battle" by Alfred Ollivant that
> Frank Cramer lent Bert. It is fine. I have been feel-
> ing like the very old scratch but for a good reason—
> one I have not told you. There is a "new arrival" on
> the way who will arrive, if no delays occur, along the
> tag end of next November.*

There it was, no wild consideration of twins, of a "little
red-headed boy" rejected by Bert, or of her own death in
childbirth. Lora, eighteen and a few months pregnant,
burdened with interminable farm chores, entered into
that spring with her childhood behind her. So occupied
was she that summer and fall that the dates of diary
entries were preceded by many stars.

> ++++++*Tuesday, June 17, 1902. It seems like I don't
> find time to write in my Journal any more.*

*++Tuesday, June 24. Dear Bert is very busy, just as
he has been, always since we came up here. Of
course there is lots of work for both of us on a ranch
but it is so nice to have Bert at home all the time.*

That summer Bert still went to lodge, but Lora had
ceased to protest since they had most of their days
together on the ranch. Lora observed in the spring of
1902:

A new lodge had been organized, Platte Valley # 34
IOOF; several clubs had appeared, among the more
popular was the Pedro Club, that card game being
very popular with practically all of the town's card-
playing citizens; the Michigan Club, organized as the
name indicates by those immigrating from Michigan.
I remember a great deal of good-natured raillery
about the "Michiganders" and the "Michigeese" was
rife. This club claimed to be the first literary club of
Encampment.... I remember a literary club, called
the Grand Encampment Literary Society, which was
organized in the log school house on the Wolfard
ranch way back in 1899....Ira Wolfard was Secretary
and signed his minutes of the meeting with a flour-
ish "IO Wolfard, Secretary GELS" and of course you
know just the nick-name that stuck to that club,
although "gels" were very scarce in camp at that
time! ...I do not think this club continued very long,
as Encampment social life soon overpowered it.

(IR, 99)

Meanwhile, Lora and Mamma had relatives,
generally Lizzie, Aunt Nan and cousins Carrie and
Maggie, for extended stays at Willow Glen. Bert
would take Lora for buggy ride outings, often to

Grand Encampment for "a little visit" to Lora's town friends or to attend an event.

++Sunday. July 6. We celebrated in great shape...I have been so tired since the dance that I scarcely know which end I am standing on.

The Fourth of July Celebration in Grand Encampment in 1902 was a very good one: Atty. Charles E Winter, "The Silver Tongued Orator" gave the address of the day. The town presented a very festive appearance, Phil Reardon having brought in several loads of Jack pines which were temporarily "planted" in front of business houses and also around a temporary park which was arranged with seats and a bandstand; this was the block—no houses there then - at the south-east corner of Freeman and Sixth. The Herald commented, "Phil is an artist and did his work in a commendable manner.

The Willis George Emerson Band put in a novel appearance as the miners band, the boys being dressed in working clothes of the typical miner.

The ball game between the Tramway Team and the Town Team resulted in a 17 to 16 victory for the Tramway Team.

In the Cow pony race, "Chub" owned by Amos Wilcox and mounted by Ted Broadwell, won first; "Teddy" owned by Frank Wilcox and mounted by himself, won second money. The sorrel mare, "Maud" mounted by Bert Bailey, won the free for all race, "Hays," Rankin's sorrel gelding winning second.

The bucking broncho [*sic*] contest was the most exciting event, several broncs being entered, all of which made the crowd scatter in all directions and do some fast scrambling to keep out of the way. The prize-winning rider was Ross Willford.

Of greatest interest to the miners was the rock drilling contest. The rock secured was the hardest granite to be found in the camp. The double-jack teams were the first called and worked as follows on fifteen minutes time.

Alex Speares and Bud Ross, 25 5/8 inches
Robert Foyle and Henry Metz, 19 3/8 inches
John Bright and Martin Aggleston, 20 7/8 inches
Davis and Stevenson, 19 7/16 inches
Duffy and Martin, 26 1/4 inches

The first prize of $125 was awarded to Duffy and Martin, the second prize of $50 to Speares and Ross.

There were three entries in the single-jack contest. E A Ross was first with 10 7/16 inches of drilling, HE Thistle second, 9 9/32 inches, John Hancock third, 5 15/16 inches. Ross received George Kuntzman's prize of $50 in gold, Thistle receiving second money, $25.00.

Carl Ashley won the boy's foot race.

The "Tug of War" between the Tramway and the Town boys resulted in a victory for the former team. Hose Co. #2 of the Encampment Fire Department made two runs, of 400 feet, one of which was made in 35 seconds. Hose Company #1 failed to show up!

The fireworks display in the evening was a pleasant feature of the program, and as the rain had interfered with the planned dancing in the open air pavilion, the school house was turned into a ball-room and dancing enjoyed until a late hour.

My husband and I who were living on my father's ranch that year, took in the celebration, and he was much surprised because I was so interested in the drilling contest. I had never seen miners drilling against time before; in fact it was only a short time before that I had seen any drilling with double-jacks. The single-jack work did not seem so amazing to me, as a man was holding his own drill, but to see a man with the drill grasped in both hands, loosen and turn that drill between mighty blows alternating from men standing one on each side of him, simply fascinated me! The first drill team I saw at work was on one of the properties managed by my husband, and one of the men wielding a double-jack was Tom Saunders. Tom was a good hard-rock miner and had very keen eye-sight, BUT he had one eye which, when he was looking north-west, appeared to be looking south-east! To see him, raining down those mighty blows and apparently looking over his shoulder while he did it, was a sight never to be forgotten. I fully expected to see him smash the hands of the man holding the drill. Later on when I mentioned to my husband, he looked surprised and said, "Oh, nobody is afraid to hold drill for Tom: he *never* misses."

(GEH/IR 116–18)

Along with caring for the kindling Belgian hares and the hatching chicks, the old log house and garden, and Bert's haying crew, Lora was sewing for baby. Encampment merchants generally furnished only the ingredients for the layette; Lora's industrious fingers had to do the rest. As she stitched, she pondered her coming role.

Monday. July 21. Mamma and Aunt Nan were to town and got some outing flannel, and this afternoon I nearly made one little night dress for baby. I am going to make three night dresses and three dresses of outing flannel (That isn't all the clothes it is to have).

++Thursday. July 24. Several days ago I went down and borrowed Nora's baby patterns and I have one little night dress made and a part of another. They are just the dearest little things. Poor dear little

baby! I am afraid it is coming to a very poor sort of a mother.

++Tuesday. Aug. 5. Lizzie is making a nice white skirt with lovely lace and insertion for it. They are all so pleased to think there is going to really be a baby in the family. I feel quite proud of myself.

Bert may have been thinking of Lora's coming confinement when he rented the ranch. Certainly her pregnancy was made more comfortable by the nearness of Mamma and the stability of living in Glen Cottage—even if the old log house was disintegrating. The pregnancy was made uncomfortable by the excessive amount of work Bert planned for her.

That summer he was not only rancher and farmer but also miner.

Sunday, July 20. This morning Bert went to town thinking to go to the Ferris–Haggarty with some men. And will not be back until late this evening or perhaps not until tomorrow. Then he is going with Frank Cramer, surveying for a few days.

++Sunday, July 27. Bert went out to Miner Creek with Mr. Burroughs the man who came up with Mr. Bohrer... Mr. Bohrer is going out this morning.

Friday Aug. 29. I am living in the hope that we will be through haying "some-day." The very last of the cutting is done now, was done this morning.

+Sunday. Aug. 31. The worst of my work is over now. Bert let both men go this evening. There is a little more hay to haul in but I think he and Dell intend to do that tomorrow. Of course I still have several things ahead of me that I intend to do. I mean extra

things. Also the choke cherries are ripe and I am
picking them "between times."

With haying behind him, Bert tackled the next ponderous fall chore; going with the team and wagon to the
timber, he began accumulating the winter woodpile. By
this time Lora noted the degeneration of his good
humor.

Monday, Sept. 15. Another utterly miserable day. To
begin, you know Mamma and I planned to go to
Lizzie's. Bert must have got up on the wrong side of
the bed, like I do so often. And he wanted to know
why I didn't ever get him anything different for
breakfast—and acted generally unpleasant all the
morning, so of course when I told him I was going to
Lizzie's, he wouldn't act decent, a bit. When I asked
him when he expected to be back, he said, "Oh, some
time between now and midnight." He asked me if I
intended to be gone all day and when I said, "yes" he
said, "O, hell!" or words to that effect. So I just
thought to myself "Well, if you want to act like a
darned bear, just go ahead" so I hiked out. When I
got to Mamma's, I found Lizzie had come over last
night and is going to stay a few days, so I stayed at
Mamma's instead but of course, all day I could not
forget how Bert had spoken to me and of course I
could not enjoy myself. So many, many times, when I
thought I was going to have a pleasant day, he had
spoiled it for me that way. I suppose it is my fault, it
<u>must</u> be but it is none the less dreadful on that
account. I wish I always knew what was right to do,
or else I wish I didn't love him quite so much. I
wouldn't care then and it wouldn't matter. And I
have tried, <u>so hard</u> to please him and do what he
wanted me to but I guess its no use. I am a very suc
cessful failure and I wish—Oh <u>how</u> I wish I'd never

married him, to try so hard and then make him miserable, but its done now and I really don't know whether he wants me to stay and keep on trying or not. It is evident that it takes something more besides "good will and awkwardness" to "keep house."

Bert's mother was informed about Lora's pregnancy. She replied, "...how pleased I am to hear you are expecting one more to love, for *a mother's love* is (to me) the sweetest thing I have ever known" (Monday, July 28). At this time "Mother," as she is denoted in Diary, was known to Lora only through her letters and her packages; she was a dispenser of gifts and advice.

Sun. Dec. 23, 1900. ...And then tonight came a box and a bundle from Bert's mother. The package contained a lovely skirt and two silk waists, one blue & one plaid for me and a <u>beautiful</u> sofa cushion for Bert that Eva made. It is just lovely, has a wreath of holly on a linen background with a red frill....

Mon. Dec. 24. 5 P.M. This morning we opened the box and found it to contain every known "goodie" under the sun, a box of bon-bons, a sack of candy, raisins, almonds, apples and oranges, two English Plum Puddings and a fruit-cake and a lot of preserved stuff.

+Tue. May 7. [1901] ... In one of Mother's letters not long ago she says, " Lora <u>you</u> are a <u>darling</u> for I know you try to make the best of things & that is the way to do. <u>Thinking</u> ourselves worse off or worse treated than other people never mends <u>anything</u> it only makes our life harder to bear, it is best to try and be as happy as possible under all circumstances & if we have our health and those <u>we love</u> to <u>love us</u>

*we have a great deal & tho our circumstances are
dull today we can hope for a bright tomorrow." Her
letters are just full of things like that and it makes
me love her more everytime I get one. I am afraid
though if she knew me she would be disappointed
for though I do as she says try to make the best of
things, as a rule, I fail most dismally....it is 8 P.M.
now, Bert is up town.*

*Oct. 28, 1901, Mon. ...I went to the ranch and found
that Lizzie had given me one of those dear little
Majolica plates that were Aunt Kate's once, by way
of a present and Mamma had got me—let me whis-
per in your ear—a bustle! To improve the shape of
my gable end so to speak. It is a fine one, made of
woven wire and I certainly do look better with it on.
I utterly demolished the dear little box of candy Bert
got for me. My! but it was good. "Sommer
Richardson's" you know and such a sweet little box.
Oh I nearly forgot to mention that last night a very
plethoric letter arrived from Mother. Upon investiga-
tion I found that it contained a sweet little handkerchief from Mother and a blue collar and tie that Eva
had made. Oh, these dear delightful people. They are
too good to me; entirely. Between them, Bert,
Mamma, Pop and Libsey, I shall be so badly spoiled
I will be unendurable....*

Mother, during Bert and Lora's courtship and early
marriage, lived in Colorado Springs with Bert's sister
Eva and her husband, Art. Eva's engagement, marriage, and subsequent pregnancy had paralled that of
her new sister-in-law Lora. Through the kindness of
Mr. Bohrer, a half-fare ticket had been arranged and
Mother was to arrive at Willow Glen for the birth of the
baby. For a time Mother's arrival was uncertain.

++*Saturday. Sept. 6. ...Tonight we heard from Mother. She can not come right away even if Mr. Bohrer can get her a ticket. Their boarder is going away on the 20th and that leaves them with a big house on their hands—and as Eva is expecting "a little visitor" in January, Mother doesn't feel like leaving her the care of it. She may be able to rent it and in that case can come.*

At any rate, Mother solved her difficulties and in a month's time arrived at Encampment and then Glen Cottage. Lora's exhausting summer was coming to an end.

++*Tuesday, Oct. 7. Last night I went to town with Bert. We did not get any word from Mother but Bert saw a man who had just come from there and lived next door to her, and he said she would be here Thursday—so that is all we know about it. I have been working pretty hard the last few days and feel pretty tired. Sunday, Papa, Dell, and Bert dug Papa's spuds and I stayed there to dinner. Yesterday I did a big washing and today baked and churned but my ironing is still ahead of me. They are digging out potatoes now and Dell eats dinner here.*

Friday, Oct. 10. Mother came last night and I am very favorably impressed with her.

Saturday. Oct. 11. Last night I got a letter from Clifford by the way, this is his twenty-second birthday. Bert was down town and got Mother's trunk and Mamma and Lizzie were up this afternoon and we all unpacked the trunk together. You know how Mother is, she always gives us so many things and of course there were lots of treasures in that trunk and she brought a nice vase for Mummy and also some nice trimmings for a waist and just lots of nice things for me, among others, half a dozen Haviland china pie plates and an olive dish, glass pitcher, some butter-chips, two vases, two sets of salt shakers, a nice wrapper and also a warm woolen wrapper, a dear little china clock, a nice bedspread, several pairs of curtains, some old silver—knives, forks & spoons, some nice table-clothes & towels, and oh, goodness knows what and dear Eva sent me a dear little kimono saque, hood & bootees that she made for baby. They are exquisite.

++Monday. Oct. 20. ...Mother and I went down to see Mamma and we sewed some. I am making baby's pinning blankets. Mother had packed in that box, a copy of Milton's poems that she got for a music prize in 1857....

Monday. Oct. 27. ...Some time soon, Bert intends to go up in the hills, to do the annual work on a claim. He said it would take him anyway a week. I don't know how I can ever get along without him for so long. One thing that has been nice about living here—he has been at home, all the time. But now when he is gone evenings I can look up and see Mother sitting opposite. It seems so nice. This dear old "room of memories" has more memories than ever now for it was here I first saw her. Bert and I were married in this room and many a happy hour we spent here before that.

Wednesday, Nov. 5. Bert went away again this morning, but he thinks he will be down Saturday—perhaps even Friday night. Lizzie and I drove to town this afternoon to get some things for Mamma. It is late now and Mother has gone to bed. I have been reading some of Bert's letters, that he has written to me since we have been married—and I love them as much as those he wrote before. They are very much the same and I love him more since he is really mine. Oh, I will be so glad when he is through with this work and so will Mother. It is really dismal for both of us, here together, as we have absolutely noth- ing in common but our love for Bert. I wish I knew how to make it pleasanter for her. I know it must be unpleasant for her, coming way off here and being with a daughter-in-law that she never saw before. God knows I am unpleasant enough at best but now I am even worse. It seems as though every little trifle vexes me so and I get so nervous, I feel crosser than two sticks and don't want any body to look at me or speak to me. But she is dear and kind and perhaps she will understand and not quite hate me.

Indeed, Mother and Lora had little in common. Her letters to Bert and Lora, in addition to advice, con- tained news of her "business schemes," "land settle- ments," and at least one lawsuit, apparently contesting the divorce settlement from her recent husband, Mr. Goldie. Years after Mother's stay with the pregnant Lora (in that fall of 1902), Lora penned in Diary a flat- tering characterization of Mother—and a bit of Oldman history.

Monday, Nov. 11, 1940, Armistice Day. Many years ago...I had my first visit from my mother-in-law, Mrs. Louise Goldie, one of the most remarkable women I have ever known. An English lady of edu- cation and refinement, about sixty years of age at that time, she had risen above circumstance throughout a life of hardship, disillusion and pover- ty, retaining through it all her sterling character, her keen appreciation of life and her fine sense of humor. I could talk for hours about her, the type of mother- in-law who makes the comic-paper jokes on the sub-

*ject merely trivial and ridiculous! Her influence on
my life was second only to that of my own dear
mother and I love and revere her memory....*

*It seems she met Mr. Goldie at her brother's
home in England where she had been offered a home
after Mr. Oldman died of tuberculosis at Detroit,
Michigan, leaving her with three small children and
no income. From her description, he must have been
a man of pleasing personality but not overly scrupu-
lous. He painted a glowing "word picture" of "his
newspaper interests" in North Carolina and the
many advantages of living in "the States." After he
returned to America, he kept up a lively correspondence with her. I think he must have been a silver
tongued orator for he finally persuaded her to come
over and marry him.*

*+++++Friday, Nov. 21. I have spent five of a very
long ten days in bed. Baby arrived at 8.45 Sunday
morning. I was only sick four hours and Dr. Perdue
gave me chloroform so I didn't really suffer at all. I
tell you it was a snap. Baby is a boy and we are
going to call him Albert Horace. Mamma has been
up every day to take care of me and dress baby. I feel
fine.*

*+++++Thanksgiving 1902, Nov. 27. I'm over at the
desk for the first time to write this. I sat up for a
while yesterday and have been up most all of today.
Papa took a freak to go to Saratoga for
Thanksgiving this year so he and Mamma went
Tuesday. I don't know when they will be back but
hope tomorrow. Lizzie is the best girl you ever saw.
She just does everything for us....Dear little sweet
baby is just too lovely for anything. Poor Mother has
worked so hard. It is just a shame but I am sure I
can't help it. When Bert went to the Ferris–Haggarty
before baby came, he bought a cook-stove and had it*

sent down on a freight team. He went to the
Ferris–Haggarty again since then and got back last
night. The Redmen are giving a swell ball tonight
and Bert has had to do all the work, as usual, and
has to go tonight too and see how things go.

Lora had a lengthy recovery period after the birth of the baby Bert. The baby cheered her days as she watched new developments around Glen Cottage and seemed to lament her inability to help Mother with the chores. Mother's stay proved to be two months in length. Upon leaving, she plied Grand Encampment's most prominent citizen to arrange for her free passage home and succeeded! Mother Goldie arrived in Colorado Springs only a month before her second grandchild, Eva's son Edgar, was born.

+Sunday, Nov. 30. Baby is two weeks old today. He
is the dearest, best baby, you ever saw, he sleeps a
great deal and very seldom cries. Eva sent him a
dear little hair-brush. It got here on the twenty-
fourth. I am getting to feel quite well and strong and
hope they let me do some work pretty soon. It is sim-
ply awful to sit here and see poor dear Mother work-
ing, working, all the time. She gets so tired, and it is
just a shame to let her work so hard and here I am
utterly unable to prevent it.

Monday, December 1, 1902. ...Bert set up my new
stove this afternoon and they opened the door
between here and the kitchen and let me look at it. It
is just a beauty. I am sure I shall like it very much.

Tuesday Dec. 2. Mother managed to work Willis
George Emerson for a pass and intends to start
home a week from today. Poor dear Mother, I am
afraid her visit has not been pleasant. Just coming

Baby Bert
In the cradle Uncle Ez gave him, in the Room of Memories.

*up here and making a galley slave of herself....Ed
and Jen are to be married on the 4th inst. Dear little
Jen, I hope she will be "so happy like nodings."
...Dear baby Bertie has slept quite a lot today. He
had a little colic this morning. It won't be long now
until I am up and doing.*

Bert became quite attentive to Lora. In addition to
the stove, he purchased another labor-saving device
and additions to the library for her pleasure.

*Friday, Dec. 5, 1902. ...Dear Hubby bought me a nice
washing machine. Isn't that nice? Mamma says "You
got lots of nice things this fall—a stove, a washing
machine, and a baby." ...Bert just sent for a set of
eight volumes of "John Kendrick Bangs" works to be*

*paid for on the installment plan. Speaking of books I
must tell you what a <u>very</u> immense library I have.
Well, to begin with, a very much be-thumbed copy of
Robinson Crusoe (which I have had since the year
1890 - then, Dickens' "Child's History of England"
which I have had nearly as long—a book called
"Christmas Stories"—"Little Women," the only one of
Louisa M. Alcott's that I have —"The Adventures of
Tom Sawyer," "Evangeline" a book by Donald G.
Mitchell called "About Old Story Tellers," "Lucile,"
"Elizabeth and her German Garden," a book pub-
lished recently anonymously, consequently creating a
stir, "The White Company" by A Conan Doyle "Blix"
by Frank K. Norris, "Black Beauty" "Story of an
African Farm" by Olive Schreiner "Twenty Thousand
Leagues Under the Sea" and "The Mysterious
Island" both by Jules Verne, "Beulah" by Augusta J.
Evans, a dear old copy of Milton's poems...a book of
poems by Longfellow, "The English Orphans" by
Mary J. Holmes and last but <u>not least</u> "David
Copperfield." There isn't that a library for your life?*

For Bert, a bright mining prospect for the winter
had evolved. This allowed him to get one more gift for
Lora .

*++Mon. Dec. 15. Bert phoned to Mr. Bohrer last
night and is to begin work on the Colorado Belle
this week. They are going to do $400 worth of work.
That will last him through January and part of
February....*

*Wednesday. Dec. 17. Yesterday I weighed baby as he
was a month old. He weighed twelve pounds. When
he was born, the doctor thought he would weigh
between nine and ten pounds. Mamma said oh she
was sure he <u>must</u> weigh ten pounds, so Bert got*

some spring scales and they weighed him. He
weighed just eight pounds, clothes and all. He has
gained a pound a week. Dear hubby got me a wed-
ding ring, by the way of a Christmas present. Our
wedding ceremony did not call for a ring but I want-
ed to have one anyway. He had said he was not
going to buy me a Christmas present, since he had
got the stove and washing machine but he "changed
his mind." They intend to go to work out on Miner
about day after tomorrow. Hank is going to work for
him. This afternoon I wrapped baby up good and
took him down to Mamma's. It was such a lovely
warm day, I thought I would take advantage of it.
Lizzie has sure got the rheumatism right and Papa
looks like a spook.

Following soon after the arrival of her son and
Bert's ardent displays of attention to her, Lora's
Christmas of 1902 should have been extraordinary; it
was, however, marred by the continuing antagonism
between Bert and Charley.

Wednesday, Dec. 24. I got my work done and then
went down to Mamma's. They gave me my presents,
as we are not going down there tomorrow. You see
Charley is there and Bert doesn't want to go, so of
course we are not going.

+Friday, Dec. 26. Yesterday Bert and I ate our dinner
in a solitary state which seemed very strange.

The photographer for the valley's children, Lora
now focused her lens on her own baby—as he lay in the
hanging basket cradle he inherited from Great-uncle
Ez. Baby Bert received many gifts. Among them, one
was most unique and one—from Papa—gave Lora special pleasure.

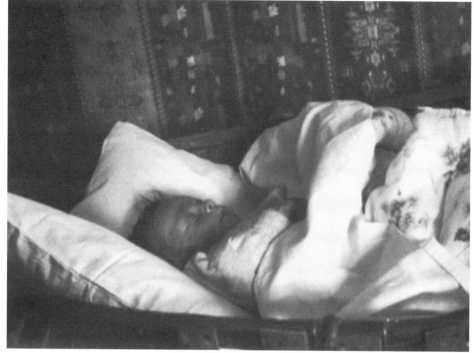

Baby Bert, close-up

At the time of Bert's birth his father was doing
work in the Encampment Copper Fields for a man
named A L Bohrer, who was head of the State
Institute for the Deaf and Blind at Colorado Springs.
Mr. Bohrer himself was blind ... and a very nice gentleman. When Bert came along, the children of the
Institute knitted the pair of little boots and sent
them. One of the pair was "wrong side out" half way;
the child knitting it had evidently got it turned
wrong side out when about half finished and merrily
finished it as though it were right side out! I gave one
to Gram and kept the other myself for years-n-years.
[letter to Vera Oldman, November 9, 1942]

Fri. Jan. 9. Mamma came up this morning and stayed until noon. When she went home, I went with her. I did some sewing I had been wanting to do. She came back up with me and carried baby. After I had been here a little while and was feeding the bunnies, I saw Pop coming up the road, wheeling the baby's carriage that had come. He did look so funny. I asked him where he was taking his baby, such a fine day, and he said out for a ride. It is a nice little buggy—one of those new fangled ones that makes into a "go cart" if you want it to. I like it very much and it was very good of "Foxy Grandpa" to get it for him.

Thursday. Jan. 15. Bert worked. I went to Mum's to dinner—was gone about an hour. It was a lovely day and baby's carriage is so nice to take him in. I took a picture of the little bunnies and tonight I developed the film, I have got one good picture of baby, asleep and the interior of the room with baby in the cradle is also good—and the bunnies too I think. Bert has gone to Lodge. Here are the pictures. Isn't he just too sweet. See his woolly head? He is sleeping on my cradle pillow, that I slept on when I was a baby. And this is part of the interior of my dear old "room of memories"—the room where he was born.

WELL, THE FAT'S IN THE FIRE NOW

WHILE LORA CONCERNED HERSELF with her pregnancy and the birth of the baby, she lost two companions of her childhood, the canary Captain Dick and her pony Nibbs. Cappy had shared the wagon on the return trip to Wyoming, had been the cohabitant of her "dear den." After her marriage to Bert, Lora moved him with her from one home to the next.

> ++*Friday, June 20. O dear! Something sad has happened. Dear little Cap is dead. I feel so bad about it but of course he couldn't live always. He was 12 years old.*

His Royal Nibbs, gift of Mr. Robbins, and "the most beautiful horse in the world" was at the ranch during Lora's confinement.

> *Friday, December 12. Poor old Nibbie wandered over from the meadow today. We really ought to have him shot but oh, I hate to. We have had such happy times together.*

Nibbs, by the Barn
"The most remarkable horse in the world"

+*Monday, January 12. ...You know I wanted Bert to have Nibbs shot, as he was past his usefulness and last night Bert told me that he had got Hank to shoot the pony some time ago so his troubles are over now. Dear little Nibbie. I had him for five years and he was very dear to me. I love horses, and especially him. Here are some pictures of him as he used to look. This is just the way he looked when I rode him with the side saddle and kept his mane roached & tail bobbed. I am so glad Bert had him shot—as we could not keep him and it is certainly no kindness to let a horse just die.*

++*Sunday, January 18. ...I will keep thinking about dear old Nibs and all the fun we had together. The eighth of last June, when I took a horseback ride*

and went over to Lib's and around over the hill
some, is the last time I ever rode him.

It was, however, the situation with Bert and
Charley that continued to destroy Lora's equanimity at
Willow Glen that winter after Baby Bert was born.

Tuesday, January 27. Well, the fats in the fire
now. Pop and Bert had a regular round-up today.
Pop called Bert all kinds of names and ended up by
telling him never to speak to him again. How it
began—Charley came up and hooked onto the sled
and drove off without so much as by your leave. He
has been doing the same thing all summer and Bert
went down to talk to Pop about it. He told Pop a few
unpleasant truths and of course Papa got mad. As
you know he doesn't like anyone to insinuate against
his way of doing.

This action by Pop could have left Bert "up against
it." Obviously, Pop's attitude called for Bert to relocate
not only Lora and the baby, but also all the farm crea-
tures Bert had gathered and were just now beginning
to produce. The previous summer, fortunately for Bert,
he had filed on a plot of land which was on the hill
above Willow Glen and close to Grand Encampment.
Lora advised Diary: "I don't know whether I ever told
you about it or not, but Bert has a fort acre desert claim
adjoining this place. He is going to put up a house on it
as he finds time and money and then we are going to
live there" (++Thursday, August 14.) Bert, with Hank
was working the winter contract job for Mr. Bohrer at
the time of Horace's blow-up. However, the new year
came in with a fury of cold and snow and halted their
work. This allowed Bert to come home and to piece
together a farmstead.

+*Friday, January 30, 1903. The weather is still bad and they have stopped work on the Colorado Belle. Bert was telling me some of the legends that Hank had pasted up about his tent, where he has been camping. On the outside he had "Hotel Freeze-out— Big Foot—Proprietor" and just inside "God damn our home" on one wall, something about Greenland's icy mountains, and Oh a lot of stuff. Bert is planning to build on "Forty Acre Farm" immediately—if Hank doesn't strike a "yob" he is going to stay and help Bert. Bert is going to build the house, move all of his rabbit pens, chicken house etc. over there get everything all ready and then we will move. Dear little Toddy-wiggle isn't very well today. it was dreadfully cold last night and he got chilled. I think and it gave him the colic. This old house is like a barn anyway. Oh, the dear old home, oh the changes, the changes, the changes,—it can never be home any more. I am glad we are going to leave it....*

+*Tuesday, February 3. Nothing in particular has happened. It snowed some more. The snow is quite deep and they are having snow slides in the mountains. in places where there never were any before. One up by the Molly Hill cabins nearly to the Golden Eagle where I used to go when Aunt Nan worked there. The hill is about / so steep - no wonder the snow slid. Comer—the man who had our house rented—and another man got buried, in one, between here and the Ferris–Haggarty and it took them several days to find their bodies. I feel so sorry for poor Mrs. Comer—They have been married only about six months.*

On Tuesday afternoon at 3.30 o'clock, a public funeral service was held at the city hall over the remains of Charles G Comer, the funeral being under the auspices of the Grand Encampment Fire Department.

Rev. Samuel Blair delivered the sermon, and hymns were sung by a large choir from the ME [Methodist–Episcopal] and Presbyterian Churches.

Dr. BE Hedding sang a baritone solo, "Rest." the fireman marched to the hall in a body, the pail bearers being Frank Lordier, Byron Tillou, Fred Watt, Peter Leffert, WA Forrest and Ed L Wood.

"Charlie" as the boys called him, was a very energetic, ambitious fellow, and became a leader in the movement to organize a fire department some months ago. He was elected Captain of Company #2 and was also Secretary of the Department. That he was esteemed by his associates in this organization is evidenced by the action of the department during the sad ordeal just passed.

The members of the Grand Encampment Fire Department did themselves proud in the kindly aid given and the interest manifested in the welfare of their comrade's bereaved wife. The action of the department has been given universal commendation.

(GEH/IR, 153–62)

+*Monday, February 9. Last night Bert telephoned to Mr. Bohrer and Mr. B is going to let him have $50 so Bert is going to start building our house immediately.*

++*Thursday, February 12. Tuesday afternoon Clella unexpectedly dropped in. She was on her way to Saratoga to file on some land and stopped to see the baby. She went on down and when she comes back is going to stop and make me a visit. Bert bought the house that Summers built up on Dell's place—for $45 and is going to move it over on our land & build on a kitchen and live there. It will not be quite such a nice looking place as he intended to build but he can nearly pay for it and so we thought it would be* *better. It will have two rooms 10x16 and then the kitchen....*

++Friday, February 13. It is frightfully cold. Having stopped storming it is freezing everything up solid.... I am so glad our sweet darling keeps well....Bert is holding him now—he says "Oh, you little Bob-nob-igan—oh there was a little boy and he was his Papa's joy and lived in Tipparari." Then he whistles. Then he says "Once there was a little jigger—and then he stops to kiss him....I hope they can get our house moved soon. Bert took down some timbers to pry with. They are going to haul it on two sets of "Bobs."

Wednesday, March 11. This was such a beautifully warm day that I took Baby-boy and went over to see our new "mansion on the square." I am simply delighted with it. Hubby dear has planned every-thing just as I like. The pantry is going to o be nice and light without any window—as the kitchen win-dow is nearly opposite it. Bert got Fred Bentley to make the window and door frames and he has done good work. I had quite a time getting over there. Could not possibly wheel baby across the creek as the snow is getting mushy and there is only a nar-row path, so I took the go-cart across first, over to the meadow where the ground is bare, and then car-ried the little boy over and put him in and wheeled him the rest of the way. Coming back I reversed the process. Dear baby did not get cold and seems to be all right.

Monday, March 23. The weather is nice again. Bert has the house all finished only the shed roof and the mop-boards in the sitting room. I have the carpet all ready to put down.... Bert has gone to town this afternoon. Our hens are laying well now. We have some to sell right along. Bert took seven dozen to town today. But he had not taken any for quite a while.

Thursday, March 26. Yesterday Bert tore down the rabbit and chicken houses. Today Dell came up and helped him and they hauled those buildings over and set them up again.... Also the churn and I made my first "batch" of butter this afternoon—about two pounds. Bert thinks that tomorrow he can get the house finished and the carpets down so that the next day we can be moving some of the things.

"Fairview Cottage" +Monday, March 30 - I guess - Am not yet sure what its name is—yesterday we moved most of our household goods over and came over ourselves. I have got the kitchen straightened up —all of the things unpacked and put into my nice big pantry. And am beginning on the sitting room now. Have both windows washed and think I can put up the curtains yet this evening. Darling baby was just as good as he could be all the while we have been moving and straightening. This morning it rained - simply poured for about an hour, then snowed a little and stopped. Has showered a little all day.

Tuesday, March 31. Still raining—o dear, o dear! Bert worked in the wet all day yesterday and today too. It is just horrid. I hope it will quit pretty soon. Ed Herring helped him today and they moved Mr. Keek—a farmer down on the river—came up and bought the calf—$7.50—only Bert is going to keep her for a few days to get the cow used to coming over here. He thinks he will move her over tomorrow, and then haul over what little hay he has left, and he will be through. He brought the cats over today and they have settled down as much at home as any-

body.... Last evening I put up the curtains in the front room and today I unpacked all of our books, our fancy dishes and bric-a-brac. Put the bed in the bed-room and got things into shape to arrange tomorrow. Got my kitchen stove all blacked beautifully. I feel pretty tired. Guess I'll go to bed. I like our lovely little home very much.

WYOMING! WYOMING!
PRECIOUS ART THOU AND THINE!

BERT'S FARMSTEAD literally appeared overnight above the sagebrush of the desert land claim. With the moving and settling in accomplished, Lora began wholeheartedly to take Baby Bert through his rites of infancy. The first transition was to move from the long dresses of infant immobility, to the short clothes of activity. At the turn of the century, both boy and girl infants were dressed the same—long and short clothes in pink and blue, with lace, ribbons, and frills.

Fri. Apr. 10. 1903. Mamma and Mrs. Shafe were up for a short while this morning. Bert finished cutting his posts and part of his poles. I have been working on boykin's short clothes this evening. I intend to put them on him tomorrow. Then I won't have a little baby any more. We had a letter from Mother this evening.

Thu. Apr. 16. Baby (you see it is still "Baby"—we haven't yet decided what to call him) is five months old today and he weighs 15 1/2 lbs. I thought he had gained more than he has he seems heavier. This morning Mamma came up and brought one of his little dresses Lizzie had finished. It is very pretty,

*made of some fine checked white goods Mother had
sent me. It has ruffles around the yoke, neck, sleeves,
and bottom. All the ruffles are edged with the prettiest little lace about so wide _____ that I had
Mamma get in town. I have not felt very well today
and dear Bert was so sweet and kind to me. He has
gone to Lodge this evening. The weather has been
quite nice for several days.*

At Fairview Cottage on the desert claim, Lora was
fairly close to the western fringe of Grand Encampment and on the path of anyone traveling in or out of
the North Fork valley or the mining country to the
West. Therefore, Lora was at the intersection of three
social sets: her relatives and country friends, her town
friends, and the miners.

*+Easter Sunday, Apr. 12. Yesterday afternoon Bert
went to town and I wheeled the baby—or rather Bert
did—almost down to the head of Freeman Ave. and
then I came back. Found that Bert had forgotten to
give me the key so I was locked out so I wheeled the
boy around for a while and then went clear to town
to see if I could see Bert. Couldn't find him so came
on back. Just as I was coming down the hill to the
house and having a good little weep over the stupidi-
ty of things in general, I met Dell who had just been
over after eggs and he came on down and got a window down from the top, went in and opened the back
door, made me a fire and was very nice. This afternoon Nora, Lindy and Annie Hickok spent the afternoon here. We had quite a chat—I haven't seen Annie
for a long time and you bet I was glad to see her.*

*Sat. May 2. Last evening John Williams came along
and kindly offered to split some wood so I was only
too willing that he should and did....This evening*

*Michael O'Conner cut some wood for us. Bert says
they are very funny—an Irishman, Mike O'Conner, a
Welshman, John Williams and an Englishman, himself. Mike is too funny for anything. He is from
Limerick and talks with a rich brogue. This evening
he met me as I was coming back from taking the boy
for a ride and he asked me why I hadn't asked him
to cut some wood. He said, "Don't ever be ashamed to
just say to me as I'm going by 'Coom herre Moike, I
want ye.'" Wouldn't that be a great way of doing
though and he said, "Why I'd brak ye oof som wood;
let us be neighborly so long as we're living neighbors." John Williams is the man that has that Placer
just above Willow Glen and Mike has some
"claimps" out here on the hill. He is staying with
John now. We give them skimmed milk every day
and one or the other comes after it...*

*Sun. May 10. Six years ago today we left Boulder—
long time isn't it? to look forward to. Mamma came
over this morning and brought the other little white
dress and the two light blue gingham slips for the
baby. This afternoon we went to town. Went and saw
Mrs. Ashley and Jen and heard Carl's new phono-
graph. They played several pretty pieces and one Jen
specially wanted me to hear and it transpired to be
"The Lost Chord." She had never heard it before.
Last night it rained all night and has showered a
little several times today. We have got a lot of young
hares they are the cutest things you ever saw....*

*+Thu. June 6. Yesterday we did some washing,
baked bread, and did various other things. Today I
took my first horse-back ride since the seventh of last
June. Think of it! I rode Bess. She is fine. Daisy
[Lora's nickname for cousin Maggie Nichols] stayed
at home and took care of Boy and also ironed all of
his little clothes while I rode to Encampment to*

Dana Merritt Houghton drawing
The Ferris–Haggarty

order some groceries. Wasn't she good? I enjoyed my ride immensely. We went to Mum's to dinner and stayed all afternoon and to supper. Shafes are camped in their yard. Shafe sold his ranch back to Jake Wagoner.

+++Tue. June 16. Saturday Daisy was sick most all day. Sunday, in the afternoon she and I went horseback, down to Uncle Ez's and back. The tram was running, and both of our horses were a little scared to go under it but they went. There was a ball-game in progress and as we came back we stopped to look on for a few minutes....Hank was here to dinner and took the horse to ride this afternoon. He brought her back this evening and he and Bert have gone to town.

Dana Merritt Houghton drawing

Across Grand Encampment, to the Smelter

The cables carrying the buckets of copper ore practically spanned the town of Grand Encampment. Any traveler afoot, with saddle horse, or team was obliged go under the tramway. The arrival of the first bucket of ore at the smelter, via the tram, was the town's most dramatic event of 1903.

TRAMWAY BRINGING ORE...BIG WORKS READY TO START

Big Demonstration Attends the Arrival of First Bucket of Ore Longest Aerial Tramway in the World is Bringing Copper Ore Over Continental Divide to Grand Encampment...16 Miles

At high noon Tuesday, June 9, 1903, the first bucket of ore carried over the aerial tramway was dumped into a bin at the big terminal at the North American Copper Company's Reduction Works in

Dana Merritt Houghton drawing
Station 3

Grand Encampment. The arrival of the bucket and its progress through the town limits enroute from the Ferris–Haggarty mine was accomplished by the booming of giant powder, the waving of flags, hats and handkerchiefs, and wild enthusiasm prevailed among a large crowd of interested people who had waited and watched for many minutes to witness the greatest event in the history of the State of Wyoming—the successful landing of ore over the longest aerial tramway in the world, the first to be built off the railroad, first in Wyoming, THE GREATEST ON THE FACE OF THE GREAT GREEN EARTH....

What a change since that day when Ed Haggarty strolled over the hills and stopped to pick up some rusty rock that had attracted his attention! Six years have lapsed since then. Great bodies move slowly, however, and Rome was not built in a day. But now the development of the camp has begun in earnest along economic business lines; now that the tramway is hauling ore to an immense new smelter at the foot of the mountains; with all the talk of railroads, etc.— what cannot another five years bring forth?

(GEH/IR 203–10)

The aerial tramway, with its moving cables and ore-filled buckets, was within sight and sound of Fairview Cottage. In later years, as part of her study of the Grand Encampment Mining District, an older Lora would be fascinated by this "greatest" of aerial tramways. But in this June of 1903, young Lora was more interested in documenting Baby Bertie's progress. She noted "boykin's" first smile, first laugh, each new tooth, each bout of cold and colic (although he was a healthy infant), every visitor, and a multitude of Bertie stories.

> *Thu. June 18. This afternoon my little Bertie and I went over to see "Grandma." ...Bert has gone to Lodge this evening. When I was down to Uncle Ez's he told me to take Bertie's clothes off in the evening and let him roll around on the bed before I put him to sleep so this evening I did and he just rolled and tumbled and laughed and enjoyed it immensely. Then I gave him some "eat" and he went right to sleep. He just gets sweeter every day.*

> *+++Wed. Aug. 26. Monday, Lizzie was up and we both spent the day at Mamma's —I was over there again yesterday. Bert and Hank have worked every day this week. Today I washed, blacked the stove, swept, dusted, washed dishes, etc. "allee samee." I am getting along quite well with Bertie's nighties. He is*

Stimson photo

The Tramway

so cute. When he wants to go anywhere now, he hitches himself along on one elbow instead of rolling, as he used to and if I sit a little way from him and hold out my hands he will come to me. A few days ago he got a sheet of sticky fly paper (which the wind must have blown out of the window) and wrapped himself up in it—well you never saw such a sight and the time I did have, getting him out of it and cleaned up again. And he laughing all the time as though it were funny.

On September 20, 1903, at the end of a lengthy entry, Lora noted, "I think perhaps there is to be another little baby at our house."

+*Fri. Oct. 9. Yesterday Bertie was pretty cross and I took him over to Mamma's as it was a nice day. About 4, I came back and Mamma came too. We found a note from Bert to the effect that he had come home and would be here to supper. Mamma had to go right back. Bert got home to supper about 7.30. My! I was glad to see him. Bertie was asleep but he woke up after a while and had some supper with us. He knew his Papa and "Goo-gooed" at him in great shape. Bert had to go back early this morning. He is getting along pretty well, with the work. He says he is going to hurry and get through as he doesn't like to be away from home. Dr. Perdue says I must wean Bertie immediately so I am. I haven't nursed him all day and am not going to any more. Poor little man! It is too pitiful. He doesn't see why he should be treated so badly.*

+*Wed. Oct. 21. Yesterday I was over at Mamma's most all day. Finished one little apron for Bertie and nearly another. Today we had quite an adventure. Lizzie wanted to go to their ranch for some things and came by here, with Colonel & the buggy to see if Bertie and I didn't want to go riding it was such a lovely day. So we went and when we had gone about a mile and a half past town the king-bolt broke and tipped us all out in the dirt. Colonel and the front axle went spinning merrily down the road and there we were. None of us were seriously hurt tho' poor little Bertie had fallen on his face and skinned his forehead the weeest [sic] bit, and he hardly cried over it at all, and I had sprained my wrist a little. We caught Colonel, and Lizzie led him home while I walked behind supporting the baby while he sat on the cross-bar of the shafts. We got to my house after a while—rather like the Kentuckian who "goeth forth in joy and gladness and cometh home in scraps and fragments," and the baby celebrated our return by sleeping for an hour and a quarter. Then we went on over to Mamma's and had dinner. I sewed some more this afternoon and came on home tonight.*

Much of the spring and summer of 1903, Bert, after seeing Lora and Bertie comfortably situated at Fairview Cottage, worked on mining claims. He contracted with C.W. Freeman for "60 days work @ $3.50 and it is only about 5 miles away so he is home nights" (+Mon. June 22, 1903). But now in September and October, he was up on the Divide near Battle for J.T. Brown and could make only infrequent trips home.

That fall the reputation of the Grand Encampment Mining District, still riding high on the completion of the aerial tramway, was elevated to greater heights by two events. The first occurred at the third annual Industrial Convention of Wyoming at Sheridan in October. The second was in November, when a world-famous showman and investor in the district made an appearance.

> Nearly all of the public officials of the state were present, including Gov. Chatterton, Senators Clark and Warren....Encampment was represented by Hon Willis Geo Emerson, Atty. Charles E Winter and Earle R Clemens of the Grand Encampment Herald, who gave his paper splendid news coverage, including the text of the Governor's speech and other matters of importance, a complete report of each day's session, prizes awarded and comments on the interest aroused by the North American Copper Co.'s blister copper display....
>
> It was at this convention that "Wyoming" was adopted as the state song. Written by Atty. Charles E Winter and set to music by Earle Clemens, it was sung in public for the first time at the convention;

written as a solo with male quartet chorus it was sung by Mr. Clemens' beautiful tenor, joined on the chorus by co-author Mr. Winter, and Messrs. Atchison and Cope of Sheridan. At the close of the convention, the song had been endorsed as the State Song by the State Press Association, the State Industrial Convention and by the faculty of the State University. Here are the five verses as originally written:

WYOMING

In the far and mighty west,
Where the crimson sun seeks rest,
There's a glowing splendid state that lies above
On the breast of this great land,
Where the massive rockies stand,
There's Wyoming, young and strong, the state I love.

In thy flowers wild and sweet,
Colors rare and perfumes meet;
There's the Columbine, so pure; the Daisy too.
Wild the Rose, and red it springs,
White the Button and its rings.
Thou art loyal, for they're red and white and blue.

Where thy peaks with crowned head,
Rising 'til the sky they wed,
Sit like snow-queens ruling wood and stream and
    plain;
'Neath thy granite bases deep,
'Neath thy bosom's broadened sweep,
Lie the riches that have gained and brought thee
    fame.

Other treasures Thou dost hold,
Men and women thou dost mould;
True and earnest are the lives that Thou dost raise.
Strength thy children Thou dost teach,

Nature's truth Thou giv'st to each,
Free and noble are thy workings and thy ways.

In the nation's banner free
There's one star that has for me
A pure radiance and a splendor like the sun;
Mine it is, Wyoming's star,
Home it leads me, near or far.
O Wyoming! All my heart and love you've won.

Chorus:
Wyoming! Wyoming! Land of the sunlight clear.
Wyoming! Wyoming! Land that we hold so dear.
Wyoming! Wyoming! Precious art Thou and thine.
Wyoming! Wyoming! Beloved state of mine."

(IR, 263–4)

"Buffalo Bill" made one of his rare visits to Encampment in November, 1903. He was returning from Europe after closing down his famous "Wild West Show." He was accompanied by Dr. Powell, his Indian blood-brother, "White Beaver." The Herald published a very complete interview with Col. Cody who always loved to talk about the progress of Wyoming, and prophesy for its future. As he came to Wyoming in 1867, he was a recognized authority. When asked whether he expected to keep his wild west show in operation, the Colonel said, "How can I drive tunnels at Grand Encampment and build canals at Cody, if I don't keep the old show going?... I have been just two weeks getting home from England, and I tell you the most enjoyable part of the trip was the ride over the sand from Walcott; it does me good to get back once more upon my old stamping grounds in Wyoming. Yes, I closed the show two weeks ago Friday night, turned loose my six hundred men and about the same number of animals, and brought two hundred of the boys home with me....

Of the boys Col. Cody brought home with him, one was an Encampment man, Joe Peryam. Good riders were common in the cattle country; all six of "the Peryam boys" were good riders, but Joe was the pick of the bunch, as the Colonel must have agreed when he was hand-picking his men to take the show to England. In the language of that early day, Joe was "part of his horse." I remember on one occasion having a splendid view of Joe's horsemanship, just in the line of his regular work; a group of valley ranchmen were bringing out cattle from the range, to their ranches for winter care. These cattle had been gathered from the hills lying between the North and South Forks of the Grand Encampment River, and some of those cattle were wild as fish-hawks! The cowboys had brought their bunch through the lane by my father's ranch, ...but after they got to the top of the hill something "spooked" them and it took expert handing to keep them grouped and traveling. One old breachy cow sailed over my father's fence into the meadow, as though she thought she was a bird. She was immediately followed by Joe, whose horse leaped the fence right after her.

At that time, I lived in a house up near the turn of the road... and from my living-room window I had practically a grand-stand seat to watch the next few minutes swift action. There was a large irrigation ditch, full to the brink and well grown up with willows on both banks. In an effort to shake her pursuer, the cow dove into the brush and for ten minutes or so, she was up one bank, down the other, around any willow bush, never pausing a moment, and right at her tail, Joe's horse, no matter where she went or how swiftly she turned. The water splashed, the willows whipped but she could not escape, and finally with a wild bellow she ran for the fence again, leaping it at a bound, and right behind her, Joe, still a part of his horse and as calm as though he were taking a tweedle-dum, tweedle-dee ride around Central Park! "Seeing daylight" between Joe and his saddle....well, it just didn't happen, that's all. If you have ever tried to get a lone "critter" out of a bunch of brush, you know how difficult it can be. That cow did a real sprint to overtake the bunch and escape that nemesis on horseback....

Upon arrival in Encampment, Col. Cody had stated that he and Col. Powell had come to visit their Copper Giant mine, as well as to take a general view of the camp. He expressed himself well pleased with the development of the entire camp and in speaking of his own mining interests, said, "Yes, I am a heavy stockholder in the Copper Giant. I am well pleased with the same and have no stock for sale. Mr. Waterbury and Col. Powell have built a magnificent tunnel, of good proportions and well-timbered, and are still driving. It is the best tunnel I have ever seen and I have seen many. The tunnel is 900 feet, with a depth almost as great as the length, and I understand it is the longest tunnel with the greatest depth in the district"....

Dr. Powell was asked to say a few words....He stated that his visit to Encampment had been pleasant in the extreme and closed by saying, "I had to bring Col. Cody here to show him that his northern Wyoming town is not in any respect ahead of this little city." One remark concerning the tramway made by Buffalo Bill during this visit has been extensively quoted. He said, "It is one of the wonderful sights of the world to see that ore moving in the air."

(GEH/IR 267–73)

At about the time of Buffalo Bill's visit, Bert was completing the work on J. T. Brown's claims near Battle.

Mon. Oct. 26. When I came home this evening, I found Bert had got through with his work and moved down. He came home to supper and went up town again afterward.

As Bert now had proved up on the desert claim, he and Lora were free to return to Cosy Cottage in the village.

Cosy Cottage, +Tue. Nov. 3. Yesterday we got our packing all finished and today we moved. Bert had spoken to Dell about moving us but Dell didn't come so Bert had to go to town and get a team & man so that gave us a very late start. They got one load hauled before noon and I put Bertie in his cart and wheeled him down. He and I went over to Belle's and had dinner which we enjoyed very much. Bert straightened up, got some dinner at the Bohn and went after another load. After dinner Belle got suddenly very sick so I went up to the Drug Store and sent Frank down and then I came on home and straightened. They got the household goods all here about five. These are busy days "foh suah." I have worked until I am almost exhausted so I am going to bed.

That winter of 1903/1904 was a season of young newlyweds and babies in the camp and in the country. Clella Fairchild had married George Brown and Nora Herring, Gene Fleming; both had been brides with Lora during the fall of 1900. Jenny Ashley, another of the belles of Encampment, was now Mrs. Ed Wood. The Wilcox girls, Belle and Edna, had married in a grand double wedding on the sixteenth of June, 1902.

...Miss Belle Wilcox became the wife of Mr. Frank J Lordier and Miss Edna Wilcox became the wife of Mr. Byron Tillou....The brides were gowned in white taffeta, while the grooms wore the traditional black. The contracting parties are among the well-known and popular young people of Grand Encampment. Mr. Lordier is a member of the Lordier–Thayer Drug Co., which enjoys a fine patronage. Mr. Tillou is employed at the Encampment Mercantile Company's store. Both are among the very early residents of the city having resided here over four years.

(GEH/IR 114)

Nora's Hazel was born in June of 1901, and Lora's Bertie followed in November of 1902. Every young mother was attentive to every other. While medical help was available at Grand Encampment, often there were no sure remedies.

+*Sat. Aug. 29. 1903. Teddie's [Edna Wilcox Tillou] baby has been very sick with cholera infantum and this morning she died. Isn't that just so sad. How they will miss her. Goodness what would we do without Bertie. Oh I am so sorry for them.*

In the fall and winter of 1903, Jen, Nora, Lora, Clella and Belle were all pregnant. Lora's social life was infant bound; on October 29 she copied in Dairy:

The Cry of the Mothers
Lizzie Clarke Hardy
My life is so narrow, so narrow,
    environed by four square walls
And ever across my threshold
    the shadow of duty falls.
My eyes wander oft to the hilltops,
    but ever my heart stoops down
In a passion of love to the babies
    that helplessly cling to my gown.

In the lights of a new day dawning
   I see an Evangel stand;
And to fields that are ripe for the harvest
   I am lured by a beckoning hand.
But I have no place with the reapers,
   no part in the soul-stirring strife
I must hover my babes on the hearth-stone
   and teach them the lessons of life.

I must answer their eager questions
   with God-given words of truth,
I must guide them in ways of wisdom
   through childhood and early youth;
I must nourish their souls and bodies
   with infinite watchful care.
Take thought of the loaves and the fishes
   and the raiment that they must wear

But at night when the lessons are over,
   and I cuddle each sleepy head,
When the questions are asked and answered and
   the last little prayer is said,
When the fruitless unrest has vanished
   that fretted my heart through the day,
Then I kneel in the midst of my children
   and humbly and thankfully pray.

Dear Lord, when I stand with the reapers
   before Thee at set of sun,
When the sheaves of the harvest are garnered
   and life and its labor is done,
I shall lay at Thy feet these, my children,
   to my heart and my garments they cling.
I may not go forth with the reapers
   but these are the sheaves I shall bring.

++*Tue. Nov. 10. Sunday afternoon we went over to
see Ed and Jen. We stayed to supper and enjoyed*

*ourselves very much. Jen showed me her baby
clothes—My! They are nice! She bought the outfit
Mrs. Pullen had for sale and then she has more
besides. Last evening Belle and Frank were over.
Bertie's little cap and mittens I sent for came yesterday. They are very nice and pretty too. Today Bert
and I cut his hair. He looks much better....*

*+++Sat. Nov. 28. ...Bertie cut a new tooth yesterday.
He has five now. His toys from M.W.& Co. came last
Wednesday. He likes them very much. I got him some
A.B.C. blocks, a bi-colored celluloid ball and a poo-
dle dog....*

*++Tue. December 1. ...Last evening Belle spent the
evening with me. We are going to make Bertie a
scrap book out of one of those Drummer's clothing-
sample books....*

*+++Sat. Dec. 5. ...Yesterday morning Jen's baby was
born. It is a girl and everything all O.K. Today
Mamma and Papa came down to dinner and stayed
quite a while. After they went Bert took the baby boy
and we went over to see Jen's baby. She is a dear little thing fat as a pig and Jen is feeling quite well.
We came on home and went down to Mrs. Holley's
but she wasn't at home so we came back.*

*++Fri. Dec. 11. Yesterday Bert went after a load of
wood. I washed and after dinner, took Bertie and we
went up town and bought some things. As I was
coming home I met Clella and George who had just
been to my house. They and Mr. and Mrs. Crout went
in one rig. Clella got out and came back. She could
only stay the least little while. Bless her old heart, I
was so glad to see her and do you know she is going
to have a baby too—next April. Grace and her baby
are with her now so she won't be so lonesome. Belle*

*was over last evening and we sewed. She was over
again this evening and we sewed more.*

Lora's friendship with Belle Lordier even held her
in Grand Encampment for the Christmas of 1903. The
Wilcox family, including Edna and Byron Tillou, had
gone to Denver for the season and Lora, rather than
following the Nichols' tradition of Christmas at the
ranch, accepted Belle's invitation.

*Thu. Dec. 24., Christmas Eve, Bert attended the mas-
querade dressed as Santa Claus. I did intend to go
and look on for a while—in fact got all dressed and
then changed my mind. It was too cold to take Bertie
and Mr. Horn (our next door neighbor) was going to
look after him while I went up and saw the masker,
but I felt so tired I decided not to go. I opened the
Christmas packages this evening and was very
delighted with the presents. Mamma and Lizzie
together gave me the dear little table teakettle that
they had sent for in the freight order. It is a beauty
nicer than any I have ever seen. The kettle and alcohol lamp are of polished brass and the frame of
wrought iron in a very handsome design. And then
Mamma got me two very handsome vegetable dishes,
which I was in great need of, and a crumb pan and
a brush. And Lizzie gave me the latest in shirtwaist
sets—"three very large pearl pins" and a beautiful
handkerchief which she <u>made</u>. Hubby darling got me
a nice bottle of perfume in a pretty box. For little
Bertie there was a silver mug, gold lined from his
Grandma and a pair of pretty little red shoes and
an <u>exquisite</u> little dress of white cashmere with a
yoke and cuffs of pink under white over-lace and
trimmed with ruffled pink ribbon—both from his
Aunt Lizzie. For Bert Mamma got a silver napkin
ring and an odd and pretty paper weight, a glass*

globe filled with shells and mounted on a china stand or base.

+*Sat. Dec. 26. "Yesterday was Christmas and every-thing was gay." We spent the entire day and evening at Lordiers and enjoyed ourselves heartily. Our din-ner was delicious. I was sick at my stomach most all day and couldn't enjoy things so much on that account. Belle surprised me by giving me a nice ebony brush and comb with sterling silver mount-ings....Today when Bert was up town Tom Smith gave him a rocking-horse for the baby. Belle was over this afternoon and Mamma and Lizzie came down too....*

THE SULPHER FUMES
HAD DONE HIM UP

WHEN BERT CAME HOME from working the mountain claims near Battle, the family moved to Grand Encampment. Bert had suspended his farm ambitions, anticipating work at the smelter for the winter; but in November, employment looked bleak.

> +*Sat. Nov. 7. Poor hubby is in a "blue funk." There is almost a certainty of the Smelter shutting down and of course that will make things deadly dull this winter.*

However, there was a job for Bert at the smelter— working night shift.

> +*Mon. Nov. 23. Bert was worn out this morning as he had not had enough sleep for two days so he went home to bed without any breakfast and didn't get up until nearly supper time. Poor hubby! It is such hard work for him. Of course I couldn't get much done only keep Bertie still...I can't use my new sewing machine while Bert is sleeping day-times. Very sad!*

Smelter Exterior *Stimson photograph*

Smelter Interior *Stimson photograph*

Tue. Nov. 24. Bert came home in the middle of the night last night; the "sulpher" fumes had done him up.

By the time of the Christmas at Lordiers, Bert was already gathering a camp outfit to return to the Colorado Belle for Mr. Bohrer. He worked claims for various investors and spent random times, whenever the ferocious winter would allow him to come down, at Cosy Cottage with Lora and Bertie.

The Herald of Jan. 15 1904, carries the front page stories of several important properties, of special interest being Harry Ball's own story of the Golden Eagle, or El Rey as it was first called. It is the oldest mine in the district and has had many difficulties and set-backs ever since it was located. Mr. Ball has always claimed the mine is hoodooed. The Itmay, Aetna, Two Toms and Blanch rated news stories, as well as the following:

SINKING WINZE
ON THE COLORADO BELLE GROUND

The Home Run Mining Co., under the supervision of AH Oldman has started work on its Colorado Belle property on Miner Creek....

The work to date upon this property consists of a tunnel 154 feet long, from which a winze has been sunk 25 feet. Several mineralized stringers were cut. It is Mr. Oldman's intention to sink the winze until a vertical depth of 100 feet from the surface has been gained, and then drift to catch the ore to which he believes the stringers are pointing. The depth obtained in the winze is now about sixty feet from the surface.

The Colorado Belle group comprises six claims, located in the early days of the camp. Mr. Oldman

Jack Ledbetter photograph
Battle Store

has great faith in the property, and states that his
company expects to furnish him ample funds to thoroughly explore the ground. The property is four miles
south of Encampment on one of the several creeks
tributary to the South Fork of the Encampment.
(GEH/IR, 276–7)

++*Mon. Jan. 25. 1904. Saturday was a very stormy
day. I cleaned my house up pretty good and about
noon while Bertie took his nap I went up to the
Mercantile Co. and ordered some groceries. Was gone
just twenty minutes. Bertie was still asleep when I
got back and slept for three quarters of an hour
afterward. He had just cut his first double tooth that
day and was pretty cross. Yesterday I got so lonesome I just didn't know what to do so after I had*

Jack Ledbetter photograph
Davy Crockett and His Dog

*mopped my kitchen and done several other things
that were not very appropriate to the Sabbath day, I
took Bertie in his carriage and went over to Belle's.
It was Frank's Sunday off so he was at home. We
stayed to dinner and quite a while afterward and
then Belle said if we would stay until after supper
she would come down with me so we stayed. Just as
we were going to sit down to supper Bert walked in*

Jack Ledbetter photograph
Families with Skis

quite to our surprise as the weather had been beastly
all the afternoon. You bet I was glad to see him....

Two Grand Encampment citizens struggled in a
mountain blizzard during that same week, and in the
words of *Herald* editor Earle Clemens "faced death for
fourteen hours."

For two weeks, Messrs. Winter and Matthews had
been waiting for good weather in order to make the
trip south from the town of Battle to measure up
some contract work on the Susquehanna property,
owned by the Standard Copper Mining Co. During
this period there had hardly been a day fit for the
trip, but on Saturday the situation looked favorable

Jack Ledbetter photograph
Horses in the Snow

as the couple started out of Grand Encampment on horseback.

As they reached the dugway in the vicinity of Battle the wind was blowing hard, driving snow from the trees into the faces of the travelers, almost blinding them, and by the time Battle was reached their eyelids were almost frozen shut. However, the sky cleared again, as if to tempt the tenderfeet on, and at one o'clock, Winter and Matthews had strapped on skees [*sic*] and started southward along the storm belt of the Sierra Madres.

Added to the inexperience of the travelers was the presence of about eight inches of new snow, through which the men trudged with slow pace making only a mile an hour. At five o'clock they were within one and one half miles of their destination, but night was rapidly coming on and the snow was falling fast....

Jack Ledbetter photograph
Sled with Women

When they could no longer travel, either by skee-
ing [*sic*] or crawling on their hands and knees, they
decided to sink a shaft and stake a snow claim for the
occasion. This was accordingly done, and with the
skees they dug a hole perhaps five feet deep and as
many long and wide. The next step was to build a
fire....The snow was fully nine feet deep—a fact later
proven—and the timber was tall and stately with but
few dry limbs....

Into this hole the two men crawled, stirring occasionally to hustle pine and rising abruptly now and
then to answer the call of their convulsive stomachs,
which were overtaxed with the taste of smoke....

The lost had hoped for a clear morning which
would have revealed to them their position, but they
were sadly disappointed....The wind was stiffer, the

snow thicker and the atmosphere sharper than the night before....

But a cabin was sighted. It was the last straw. The men were encouraged and struggled on only to find that the cabin was a deserted stable, with an open door and snowed full to the roof....

Matthews was ahead and in five minutes sighted more cabins. They had struck Rambler, and staggering into the rear door of Scott's Hotel they embraced the "Smiling face of Joe Inkhouse, which," said Winter, "never looked more angelic to me before. Talk about the holy city," continued Winter, "Rambler looked plenty good enough to me."

(GEH/IR, 277–82)

In addition to the extensive article concerning the near fatal adventure, Clemens, Winter's co-author of the state song "Wyoming," continued in an editorial to stress the dangers blizzards posed to both pioneer and tenderfoot. He concluded with a recipe for winter travel in the Grand Encampment Mining District; "...men should carry at least the following: a compass, three days' grub, small bottle of kerosene and an elephant's nerve." (GEH/IR, 283)

+*Sat. Feb. 20. ...Tonight Bert heard from a contract he had bid on and his terms are accepted ($9.00 per foot on a 100 ft. tunnel starting at the surface.) so he will go to work on that as soon as he gets back from his trip. He intends to go on to Colorado Springs while he is so near. I think it will be so nice for him. He can see Eva and her baby and the rest and stay a few days with them.*

+++*Wed. Feb. 24. Monday morning Bert took the stage for Cheyenne. He is going on to Colorado*

Springs to see his folks before he comes back. I went up to the ranch that same day. Was down yesterday after some things and down again today after more things.

+++Sun. Feb. 28. ...Bert is in Colorado Springs now. His letter is dated 26 Feb. and he says,

My Darling Wife,

Here I am safe and sound and enjoying life, you bet, the weather is just ideal, about like our June.

I have been to two or three Vaudeville shows and went to a dance for an hour or so, had just two dances, the floor was elegant, also the music, but partners were scarce, at least for me.

All the family here are fairly well, Eva is not feeling first-rate.

I saw the two Wilcox boys on the street in Denver they were dressed right up to date and were quite swell.

Colorado Springs has improved so much in the past five years that I hardly know the place, as I write, I have a pink carnation larger round than a dollar in my button-hole, I bought it for 5¢. I hope you and the dear boy are well, kiss little Bert for me. I expect to leave here for home, Tuesday the 2nd of March, may get home Wednesday but will be there Thursday, sure. Little Edgar is running around in his walking machine and making a great racket. He is a fine large boy much heavier than little Bert but not nearly as far advanced, he is a sweet little fellow, Eva and Art have such a pretty little home.

Lots of love my darling
from
Your Own
Bert

Across the top of the letter, Mother had written "Such a happy <u>surprise</u> to see Bert come—lots of love for you darling from Mother."

ALL THAT HOLDS WYOMING TOGETHER
IS BALING WIRE AND CAPABLE WOMEN

As LORA'S PREGNANCY PROGRESSED, she felt increasingly "wretched." She anticipated that the new baby would arrive in the middle of May and thus join the lengthening list of that year's newborns.

++Fri. Apr. 1. Nora's baby arrived Wednesday morning. Another girl...On Wednesday, Mrs. Leffert and Mrs. Horn and her baby came to see me.

Sat. Apr. 2. Had a letter from Clella last night. She says my little daughter-in-law's name is to be Myrtle.

Wed. Apr. 13. Last night I received a letter from Clella dated the 9th. On which was the following post-script in George's hand.

Clella and Myrtle have been resting very quietly since 6 o'clock this beautiful morning. *Myrtle* is a fine healthy looking *Boy* weighing 9 lbs. He sends best regards to his Aunt Lora and Uncle Bert. 4–11–04...

Baby Bert, in pram

Burdened with Bertie and the constant moving between Cozy Cottage and the ranch, Lora moved to Mamma's to await her delivery.

+++Mon. Apr. 11, Glen Cottage. Friday I felt so bad Bert went to get Mamma. Just a little while before she came, Lizzie came over. Had come to help me what she could. She stayed all day and did a lot for me. Daisy was there to dinner. Mamma stayed all that day and night and the next day we availed ourselves of their invitation to come up to the ranch and stay a while. That being more convenient to them, on account of the cow. Today Papa and Bert went down

and got our chickens and brought them up here. I went with them and got some more things I wanted....

Sat. Apr. 16. The weather isn't quite so nice today as it has been. The wind is blowing. Bert has been laid up all morning with a headache. After dinner he and Papa fixed the pump which was "out of whack" and then he went to town. He came back up to supper but had to go down again as he had forgotten to mail his letters. It is very nice to be up here with my Mamma when I feel so miserable. If I don't feel like working why I don't just have to keep at it anyway, and then I don't get so lonesome. Bert says the company will start work pretty soon. I don't know whether I will stay here until my baby comes or whether Bert's Mother will come up or how it will be. I hope it will be a nice day tomorrow so Bertie can play out of doors. It was too cold this afternoon and we had to keep him in. He didn't like it a bit either. He is seventeen months old today.

+++++++++++Thu. May 19th. Sunday morning the 8th, I was taken sick about 5 o'clock. Bert went for the Doctor at once and he gave me chloroform as soon as he came. The baby was born at 11.30. A six pound girl. She came very near not living. She cried at first but stopped breathing two different times and they had to throw cold water over her and slap her and work with her about ten minutes before they got her to breathing right. She has been doing fine ever since though. The day after the baby was born, Uncle Ez and Maggie were up, and we hired Maggie to come up and help us a week. Wednesday a week ago, Mr. Fehringer came up and the next evening he and Bert went up to the claims. Friday I was taken with a very bad attack of piles and in the night I got to suffering such agonies that Papa got up and went

for the Doctor. He soon relieved the pain when he came and has come up once a day since and sometimes twice. Saturday evening I had quite an attack of fever and when Papa was down for the Doctor he saw Lizzie and Charley in town and Lizzie just came right up with him. Charley had said as soon as they heard of it— (they were over for a few minutes a day or so after the baby was born) that he would spare her to us if we needed her, though he is still in the midst of potato planting. Got a man helping him and he would have to batch without her. I think it was real kind of him. Sunday about noon, Aunt Nan and Uncle Platt came up. They stayed all night and went home again early the next morning. The Doctor said the bowel trouble was not caused by the confinement at all but that my being in a weakened condition it will naturally retard my recovery. And O for the love of Mike, he is keeping me on a light diet of beef-tea, oat-meal, etc., and I feel like a very hungry pig trying to live on thin dish water. And he says it will be anyway five more days before I can get up.

++++++Wed. June 1. On Monday I was allowed to sit up and though I was quite weak, I am getting a bit stronger now. Lizzie went home yesterday. Daisy is still here. Saturday Bert went over to Pearl with Ed Drury to see about sorting some ore. He came back the next day and told Drury that if I got up all right he would be ready to go back in a few days. He intends to go tomorrow. The baby is doing pretty well tho' she has colic a good deal. Bertie's stomach teeth are starting and he is pretty cross.

+++Tue. June 7. Sunday Daisy went home, and yesterday Lizzie came over to stay while Charley goes for a load of coal. Today Mrs. Parr and Clara took dinner with us. I am getting better right along. Have

Bert with Grandpa, on Little Colonel

taken care of the baby for the last three nights. She doesn't have colic so bad now. We had Frank mix her up some Anise Water and it helped her. Bertie has been pretty good. Goes out and picks flowers and has a good time.

++Wed. June 15. Yesterday Bert went up to start work on the Home Runs. He says he will be down in two weeks, and perhaps in one. Yesterday I went over to our house and got some things I wanted. Today Papa went fishing over to the mouth of Beaver and Mamma went with him. I kept house all day with the two babies to see how I got along. Bertie was very good and so was the baby so I did fine. We call the baby Sylvia Louise. I think we will call her Lou or Louie. She is getting fat as a little pig and don't have the colic so bad any more. In about a month if I

feel strong enough and everything is favorable I will take the babies and go up where Bert is.

+Fri. July 29. ...I walked to town this afternoon and got a letter from Mother. She says "I am so glad your dear baby is so good (I am going to call her <u>Sylvia</u>, she must be called your <u>dear, good, kind Mother's name</u> & please <u>don't</u> call her <u>after me</u>, and <u>I don't like</u> the name of Louie <u>at all</u>." So I guess we will call her Sylvia I wanted to all the time but thought she would like to have the baby called after <u>her</u>. I am sure I don't need any one to tell me how dear and good and kind my Mother is for no one knows it better.

As it evolved, Lora did not go to the hills with Bert but stayed at the ranch. Although Lora had recovered from her confinement, Sylvia continued to have intermittent colic and Bertie was fussy with his teething. Not only were Mamma and Lizzie present, but an attentive stream of visitors passed through Willow Glen. Lora could enjoy "both babies" and revive some neglected other, older interests.

Fri. Aug. 19. This forenoon I rode (horseback) to town with Bert and we went down and looked at our house. The people who had it rented have moved out and everything is in good shape. Saw Mayme for a few minutes. This afternoon Bert went back up in the hills and I rode with him part way. It is a real treat to me to go horseback riding and know that the babies are being taken care of. Bert thinks that the Co. may work for most of the winter. I hope they will.

Mon. Aug. 22. I went to town today—and got a cute little platter or rather two and I am going to save one for Lizzie's Christmas. Took Bertie with me and

Mr. Forrest gave me some candy. (I mostly get Mamma's groceries at Parkinson's) This afternoon Mamma, Bertie and I went up to the old garden and picked currants. Bertie says," Oh, pitty-pums!" and pranced all around the bush and picked all the while we did. He always calls fruit of any kind, plums. There is a service berry bush in the garden and every time Mamma picks any he says "Make pie!" I had to go to town again this evening and I took him along. Dear little Sylvia has been very good of late and she is getting so sweet and dear. She will laugh when we talk to her, and knows my voice perfectly. Wish I could see dear old Bert. Perhaps I will get a letter tomorrow night.

+Fri. Sept. 2. Today we took a picture of Sylvia sitting in her Grandfather's big chair. Daisy was here to dinner. This forenoon Mamma, Lizzie and I spent in putting up pickles. In the afternoon Lizzie and I took little Bert and drove Prince to town. I got some printing paper, toner, film, etc., from Frank, but he didn't have any developer so I couldn't develope any film tonight....

During the spring, Bert had been briefly out of a job because of a miners' strike in the Ferris–Haggarty District (Tuesday, August 23). He used the few days of the strike to look at land in the Big Creek country, where Clella and George Brown lived. Then in October, he was thinking of buying a ranch nearer Encampment. For Bert and others, perhaps the promise of the mining district was fading.

Fri. Aug. 26. Belle's baby was born this afternoon. It is a boy. Tomorrow Bert intends to go over to Big Creek again and take a surveyor. On their trip yes-

terday he shot ten sage chickens and enjoyed himself hugely.

Tue. Oct. 4. I have been printing pictures to make stereoscope views of this morning, and I find that I have a great many negatives that are "out of sight" for that purpose. Mamma and I sent for some calling cards not long ago and last night they came. They are very nice. Bert thinks he will have to stay up there a whole month this time. The Company may shut down at the end of that time and then we will go to housekeeping again. Bert wants to buy the Wood place down near Uncle Ez's, if his Mother can put up part of the money. (She wants to go in with him and buy a place somewhere.) He phoned to her and she says she will write to him about it. Wood wants $1500 and if she can put in $500 he can raise the rest. We think that much better than the other, so far away and then this is fenced & has a good house on it.

One Name Will Do

There is a general disposition among the business men of the city to drop the "Grand" and use only "Encampment" in designating the name of the Denver of Wyoming....

Until the matter is settled, officially, let those who believe that there is more virtue in one name for this enterprising town to designate it as Encampment, using Encampment on stationery, advertisements, prospectuses, etc. and using every influence to bring about a universal understanding that there is only one Encampment in Wyoming. It is Grand to be sure, but it has been in existence long enough so that we need not say so any longer.

Henceforth, we live in and for Encampment, the greatest, grandest town in the state of Wyoming!

(GEH/IR, 304–5)

Although in the fall of 1904 hopes still ran high for Encampment's future, the big Goldfield excitement in Nevada had drawn many from Encampment to look for the pot of gold—or should I say COPPER?— at the rainbow's end....

Ed Haggarty had gone to Goldfield early in the fall and Earle Clemens was already there, or rather at Rhyolite where he had established a newspaper. When the newspapers of a camp start deserting, what next?...

Notwithstanding the fact that many more Encampment mines were working, Nevada contin- ued to draw many men from this district. The Charter Oak, one of the oldest mines in camp, origi- nally located by Jones and Williams of Cow Creek, began working again in June 1904 and in late September of that year they started shipping to the smelter at Encampment. The Portland, at Battle, worked all winter in 1904-05 and was producing for the next few years. In the fall of 1904 copper was worth 13 or 14 cents a pound.

The Rawlins–Dillon Stage line discontinued in April of 04 for lack of patrons. In October the post office at Riverside was discontinued....

The Dillon Doublejack reported on properties in the vicinity: A H Oldman prosecuting work steadily on the Home Run shaft; Pluto doing 300 feet more work, under contract,; the Emerald Queen working a crew of 14 in mining operations and the erection of a large mess house and bunk house with a view to working through the winter. Several properties in various parts of camp were increasing their holdings, due mostly to recently made gold strikes near Dillon....

Transportation was still a big problem for the camp. With all the talk of a railroad to Encampment in the near future, nothing definite was done. The general opinion seemed to be that the railroad from Laramie coming through by way of Centennial would be the first to reach Encampment....

The Cheyenne Leader, as the Herald of Oct. 28, 1904 says, quoted Col. J K Jeffries of the Union Pacific, who stopped in Cheyenne briefly on his way from Denver to his home at Dillon. Col. Jeffries said, "All the large mining properties in the Battle Lake district are to be worked during the winter. ...Encampment, Dillon, Battle and Rambler all are thriving towns and there is no talk of business slackness in any of them....There is little doubt in my mind that the Union Pacific before long will build a branch line through Saratoga to Encampment."

(GEH/IR 305–8)

In September 1904 when the railroad was mostly a matter of "Hope deferred" as one merchant expressed it, it is not surprising that the town's socialites—that fun loving bunch—just up and had a first train of their own. *The Herald* of September 9 gives the story:

ENTERTAINED IN A NOVEL WAY
First Railroad Train in Encampment Carried a Jolly Crew of About Sixty Souls

The "Go Slow and Never Arrive Railroad" made its initial trip Tuesday evening at 8.30 o'clock. It was indeed much in evidence during the hours of darkness, but faded with the morn as many of Encampment's railroad dreams have done.

The first train moved in two sections, starting from the residence of Mr. and Mrs. George Kuntzman, stopping at Allentown, Phillipsburg, and Ferreeport. The power motive consisted of livery teams and the coaches were some relation to hayracks or alfalfa carryalls.

The passengers were not allowed to wear their own clothes. That fact doubtless accounted for the misfits present and the liberal picking of pockets which was a prevailing feature of the trip.

George Washington was there, and Si Plunkett was not absent. Some of the boys and girls 'we used to know' were again in their old form; indeed it was a funny bunch, that first crew of the first railroad trip in Encampment.

George Kuntzman sold the tickets. Carl Ashley and Wayne Phillips as the colored porters rustled the baggage, and SE Ferree, who was tagged so that he would not be lost, acted as baggage-master. E C Allen, as newsboy, was offering the Grand Encampment Herald to all suspicious characters.

Boarding the train, the two sections moved through the crowded streets of the city and pulled up at the home of Mr. and Mrs. E C Allen, where the red light of a way station was hung out. In the depot of this station the passengers were trying to figure out the silhouettes which lined the walls, Mrs. Butler being the most successful contestant.

Punch was served without thought of the great expense of filling the thirsty bunch, and when the punch was gone the trains tooted and away they went to the home of Mr. and Mrs. JE Phillips. On the way a daring hold-up was made, but armed tourists succeeded after a desperate fight in frightening the robbers away.

It was discovered that half of the passengers were from Frisco and the other half from Chicago.

> Wah, hoo wah,
> Hoo, wah, hoo.
> We are Friscos,
> Who are you?

> Rah, rah, rah,
> Sizz, bah, boom;
> We are Chicago
> Give us room.

The tourists lined up for athletic sports. The high kick, shot put and hammer throw were indulged in, and the honors were about even, winners being as follows: High jump, Mrs. Butler; shot put, Rev. Murray; hammer throw, Mrs. Ashley.

The train tooted again and Ferreeport was sighted. The tourists, wearied of long hours of pleasure and sight-seeing, gaming and contesting, were compelled to eat a sumptuous repast, and none objected....The prize winners were announced and all dispersed for the night, voting a most excellent trip where hospitality, fun, and noise reigned supreme.

(GEH/IR, 327–8)

Bert, this October of 1904, still had a job with the Company, Mr. Bohrer and his associates. Like others dependent upon the success of the Grand Encampment District, he had the same questions. Would the promise of the claims be realized? Would copper prices hold? Should he look for a new livelihood to support himself, Lora and the babies? Was the railroad actually coming? As the passengers on Encampment's first train found solace in conviviality, so Bert and Lora found solace in a stroll through town. It began with the arrival of an extraordinary trunk from Mother.

Wed. Oct. 12. Now I will try and tell about the things in the trunk (which was very acceptable in itself). There was a suit of clothes for Bert,—sort of a gray and very pretty, I thought—and a lot of shirts & ties—all very pretty. Also two hats but I can't tell anything about them until I see them on him. There were two pair of gloves for him—a dress pair and one fleece lined. And then for Bertie two little wash suits, two pair of shoes, very nice—a dear little blue jacket, trimmed in braid & brass buttons, a blue cloth cap to match, a little leather cap which is too

cute for anything, a lovely gray "Astrakhan" tam,
four or five pairs of stockings (There were also two
pairs of nice sox & some hdkfs [handkerchiefs] for
Bert) and for the baby a <u>beautiful</u> little white coat, a
pair of little tan shoes, a dear little warm white
hood, several pairs of stockings and a rubber ball
and a rubber doll. For me, a fine cloak, dark gray,
rough goods and fits fine, a gray hat with a blue
plume, and a hem-stitched <u>shaded</u> blue veil, gray
silk gloves. A golf cap and golf gloves. A beautiful
white waist and a tan with blue dots—both look
well on me. Some pretty aprons. Two nice skirts, one
gray, one blue, both <u>very nice</u> and a nice mercerized
black petticoat, five pairs stockings and some hdkfs.
a beautiful lace collar, and some lovely ribbons, some
new combs for my hair. And one of the latest in
handbags (They call them "Peggy from Paris") and
inside there are two pockets one containing a pocket-
book & one a card case to match the bag....

+Wed. Nov. 2. Bert came down Monday night—
walked in, in the middle of the night and surprised
me. He stayed over yesterday, and we put on our
swellest new clothes and went to town. As it was
warm & sunny we took the baby. I did enjoy going
out with Bert once more. He thought all the new
things were as nice as I felt sure he would. His
clothes fit him <u>beautifully</u>, as though they had been
<u>made</u> for him and he looks so nice in them. He came
home <u>early</u> last night and spent the evening with us.
He had to go back today. They don't know <u>yet</u>
whether they will work all winter or not. He is to
know in a week or ten days. So we are as unsettled
as ever. He gave me money to send and have my
watch fixed which is to be my birthday and
Christmas present.

In November of 1904, Lora, teenage bride and now young mother of Bertie and Sylvia, participated in another ritual of passage.

'LECTION ECHO

Woman suffrage is the text
Of many sermons, speeches, talks;
But when woman's given suffrage—
Do you know—there's where she balks.

Women say they want to vote,
But when the chance is given,
At least one-half refuse and say:
"Voting's not for women."

Now stubbornness may be a fault
Or a redeeming feature;
But anyway a woman is
A mighty funny creature.

What she has not, that she wants,
What she has don't fill the bill;
But just the same we can't complain—
"With all her faults we love her still."
(Earle Clemens in the GEH/IR, 112–13)

Wed. Nov. 9, 1904. Yesterday was election day & we all rode down in one of the "Campaign" wagons and voted....

Nov. 11, 1904, *Herald,* in its editorial columns comments: "There were several 'first' votes cast among the ladies last Tuesday and some very amusing things happened. One lady wrote her name on the outside of the ticket; another came out of the booth with her ticket unfolded; another got so excited that she tore the ticket into two parts so that a new one had to be substituted; and yet, every vote counted, and the fact is, barring a few incidents as above, the ladies of Encampment showed just as much intelligence with the ballot as the men, and perhaps on the average a little more so."

I cast my own "first" ballot that year, for "Teddy": I hope none of the above blunders was made by me...I felt very important, being a voter..

(Lora in IR, 343)

INDEX